BOOK

OF

ONE'S

OWN

Turning your family history,
travel journal, memoirs,
children's story, poetry, novel,
recipes or self-help guide
into a book.

SUSAN YATES
GREG IOANNOU

M&S

A Bloomington Book published by McClelland & Stewart.

Canadian Cataloguing in Publication Data

Yates, Susan
    A book of one's own : turning your family history, travel journal, memoirs, children's story, poetry, novel, recipes or self-help guide into a book
    Includes index.

ISBN 0-7710-9063-3

I. Self-publishing. I. Ioannou, Gregory Phillip, 1953-
II. Title.

Z285.5.Y38 1999   070.5'93   C99 900217-1

We acknowledge the financial support of the Government of Canada through the Book Publishing Development Program for our publishing activities. We further acknowledge the support of the Canada Council for the Arts for our publishing program.

Dedication
For Niles, Tap, Mom and Dad, with love. SY
For Anne, Seth and Leah, also with love. GI

McClelland & Stewart Inc.
The Canadian Publishers
481 University Avenue
Toronto, Ontario
M5G 2E9

Printed and bound in Canada

1 2 3 4 5 03 02 01 00 99

CONTENTS

ACKNOWLEDGMENTS

Thanks to the many experts who lent their valuable time. They especially include Brant Cowie, Paul Payer and Dave Murphy, ArtPlus Design and Communications; Frank Prest, Transcontinental Printing; Andrew Smith and Joseph Gisini, Andrew Smith Design; Paul Sushycki, Gandalf; and Wendy Thomas. Many thanks to the crew at Colborne Communications: Marie-Lynn Hammond, Leah McLaren, Dennis Mills, Laura Siberry, Ilana Weitzman and Wendy Yano. Special thanks also to everyone at McClelland & Stewart.

CHAPTER 1

SO THE PUBLISHERS TURNED YOU DOWN...

Most people who want to publish a book follow a pretty traditional route: They write the manuscript and send it to agents or publishers, who send it straight back. It is an easy, if depressing, way to accumulate a fine collection of rejection letters.

There is another way, however, one that is open to more and more people, particularly because new technologies are making it cheaper and easier: publishing it yourself. This book explores the various ways of doing just that. We can help you publish your book, whether it is intended to be the Next Great Novel, a family history prepared for a handful of close relatives, or a book of poems you've been polishing for years.

Although we will discuss how publishing companies assess books and what they sign, this book is designed for people who want to do it themselves, especially those whose publishing projects are on a small scale. Rather than using the term "self-publishing," which has connotations of "no one wanted to publish the thing so I just did it myself," we've used "home publishing," to reflect the fact that most publishing projects outside of the mainstream book publishing industry are small-scale labours of love.

Your book can be hand-made or professionally bound, can be handwritten or elaborately typeset. You can tailor the look — and the cost — to your particular needs and the needs of your readers. This book will lead you through the various options.

People will find this book useful if they want to publish:

- a family history
- a school yearbook
- a book about a hobby
- poetry
- seminar or workshop handouts
- a book for a religious group
- a local history
- their memoirs
- a book from an unpopular or unconventional viewpoint
- a cookbook
- a book of musings (or a rant) on how to improve the world
- a book to be sold in a fund-raising effort
- a book intended to promote a business
- an experimental novel
- a book on a topic that is so off-beat that traditional publishers aren't interested

People who don't need this book:

- Tom Clancy

WHY DO YOU WANT TO PUBLISH A BOOK?

But first things first. Let's ask some of the questions that publishers will ask of your manuscript. They are questions that need to be asked of any publishing project.

What Are You Trying to Communicate?

Many publishing projects never get off the ground because they have no central idea, or because there is no market for that central idea. Until that central idea has been thought through clearly, there is no point even starting to write the book. Many publishing projects should be shot down before they start, because the writer has no particular reason (other than ego gratification) for writing the book.

A book with a weak central idea can often be improved by recasting that idea. For example, imagine that you are a twenty-year-old university student, and you have your heart set on writing a cookbook. You pull together your favourite recipes and send them off to a publisher. A book whose central theme is "the favourite recipes of a twenty-year-old that no one has ever heard of" has very little sales potential. Rethink it a bit, and you might come up with "simple recipes any university student can cook," and you have the glimmerings of a commercial project. Keep thinking, and you might come up with "dine like royalty on a student's budget" and you have a project with some definite sales potential. They may well be exactly the same recipes, but they are now tied together by a unifying theme.

Who Will Buy the Book?

Traditional publishers take three approaches to defining the audience for a book:

- they look for books that will reach their house's usual audience (for example, the editors at Harlequin look for manuscripts that exactly fit their fiction lines);
- they aim for a clearly definable readership (such as "readers of hockey books"); or
- they try for the biggest audience they can.

If you are publishing it yourself, you aren't necessarily constrained by the need to sell a huge number of copies, but — if you want to sell your book at all — you do need to think through how many copies you are likely to sell, who you will sell them to, and how to reach that readership.

Is a Book the Right Vehicle?

Books have enormous strengths and terrible weaknesses. Is there enough material for a book? Is a book the right format to get that material into your target audience's hands? You might, for example, find that you can more effectively reach the same audience by publishing a shorter version of your material in a magazine.

Books' Strengths	Books' Weaknesses
• durable – can last for centuries	• difficult to update and revise
• inexpensive if printed in sufficient quantities	• can be expensive in small quantities
• portable	• heavy and bulky in quantity
• impressive if designed and edited well	• mortifying if poorly done
• long – enough space to thoroughly explore an idea or topic	• long – can seem endless if the idea or topic was more suited to a magazine article
• will impress some potential customers	• will intimidate some potential customers
• a potentially inexpensive way to reach many readers	• other modes of communication can be cheaper

Can You Write?

You're probably the wrong person to ask. Many wonderful writers are too aware of their shortcomings, and many awful writers are unaware that they have any shortcomings.

But the writing quality of the original manuscript is a factor in any publishing project. Publishers are willing to pay the costs of polishing a manuscript, but they sometimes make the decision on whether or not to publish after analyzing editorial costs. You probably should do likewise, unless your project is intended to stay within your family or a small circle of friends.

Will it Make Money?

If your publication is intended to make money, pay careful attention to the discussion of budgeting in Chapter 3. Even if you aren't intending to make a profit, you should keep a careful watch on your costs. This book will let you know the likely costs before you get too deeply committed to the project.

How Risky is It?

The classic failed home-publishing venture costs far more than the publisher expected, and brings in far less revenue. Often the net result is a thinner bank account and a basement full of books. We'll try to lead you to ways to save money and keep a lid on costs, but it's harder to fill in the other side of the equation for you. Many home-publishing ventures bring in only a small fraction of the publisher's most pessimistic income projection. To be safe, when you calculate your projected sales, assume the worst — and be honest with yourself. Then, when you are doing a final budget, use half of that worst-case income projection. If the project still makes financial sense, go ahead!

HAVE YOU REALLY COVERED ALL THE BASES?

You might have noticed that this book isn't home-published. Did you wonder why?

If you publish with a traditional publisher, the publisher pays you for the right to publish your manuscript and pays all the costs of producing the book. The publisher assumes all of the risks.

When you do it yourself, you pay all of the costs, and all of the risk is yours. You only get paid, if at all, when people start buying your book.

Most important of all, traditional publishers' most essential area of expertise is distribution — getting the book into the hands of potential buyers. Problems with distribution makes most home-publishing ventures unprofitable.

So, given the choice between going with someone who was willing to take all the risks and pay us to produce the book, or taking all of the risks and paying for everything ourselves, we took the money.

And so should you. It makes no sense to publish something yourself if a reputable traditional publisher is willing to do it for you. It also makes no sense to decide to do it yourself before you've thoroughly explored the possibility of finding a traditional publisher for your project.

You say you've tried the traditional publishing firms, with no luck. Were you persistent enough? Many people get discouraged when their manuscript has been rejected by a handful of publishers. If you'd really rather have your book published by a publishing firm, you may have to be very dogged. It is common for a manuscript to be rejected 10, 20 or 50 times before it finds a home.

WHERE TO FIND INFORMATION ON BOOK PUBLISHERS

If you're trying to find a publisher, don't just send out copies of your manuscript indiscriminately. Make sure that the places you are sending it to actually publish that kind of book, and find out whether they accept unsolicited manuscripts. Most publishers don't — but most are happy to be approached by means of a query letter, which we'll explain in Chapter 2. The following books give information on publishers and their submission requirements. Most are published annually.

Weller, Adrian. *The Canadian Writer's Market.* Toronto: McClelland & Stewart.

Kerner, Fred, Ed. *The Canadian Writer's Guide.* Richmond Hill: Fitzhenry & Whiteside Ltd.

Herman, Jeff. *Writer's Guide to Book Editors, Publishers, and Literary Agents.* Rocklin: Prima Publishing.

Behrens, Matthew, Ed. *The Canadian Publishers Directory.* Toronto: Quill & Quire, seasonal (with subscription; most libraries have a copy).

Holm, Kirsten, Ed. *Writer's Market.* Cincinnati: Writer's Digest Books. (Provides information on publishers in the United States.)

So Why Would Anyone of Sound Mind Consider Home Publishing?

The traditional publishers will pay you for your manuscript and promote it professionally. Do it yourself and you get all of the costs and potentially huge hassles. Why bother? For all sorts of good reasons.

"The odds." A major Canadian publisher estimated a few years ago that there were about 200,000 English-language manuscripts doing the rounds of Canadian publishers. Ten times as many are circulating in the U.S. Fewer than 1% of those will ever find a publisher.

Most people who want to write a book have little choice but to publish it themselves if they want to see it in print.

HOW PUBLISHERS COPE WITH THE FLOOD OF MANUSCRIPTS

You work for a big publisher, and are far too aware of those thousands of manuscripts trying to find a home. How do you keep the deluge from overwhelming you? The three main strategies are:

1. Accepting no unsolicited manuscripts whatsoever.

1. Accepting manuscripts only from agents, thereby redirecting the flood to the poor agents.

3. Accepting only query letters, and asking to see samples from only the very few whose query letters pique your interest.

Low overhead and lower break-even point. Many perfectly wonderful home-publishing projects just aren't financially viable for book publishing firms. A local history that will sell only 200 copies is unlikely to appeal to even the smallest small press (unless it came with a grant of some sort to publish it), but can make a worthwhile home-publishing venture, because the home publisher doesn't have to carry all of the overhead of trying to produce and distribute a full list of books. Printing 200 copies of that local history book and distributing them to the members of a local history society can make considerable financial sense.

Flexibility. Want to produce a handbook that can be printed in tiny quantities and updated every month or two? Traditional publishing doesn't want to know you exist.

Creativity. Want your poetry book to have a hand-embossed cover, handmade paper pages, and a creatively stitched binding? You may well have the time available to invest in producing such a labour of love. The big publisher doesn't. Sometimes you are the only person who can give a project the love and care it deserves.

Control. Talk to many writers, and they'll tell you: "People thought my book of poetry was a Harlequin with that cover they put on it"; "Why did they change the name of my book to *Attack of the Aardvark Lizards*? What was wrong with *Green Sticky Things?*"; and "The page design is so confusing I can't even find the page numbers."

Publish it yourself and it will come out the way you wanted it to (give or take your own abilities and budget, and if the printers are willing!).

These last two factors are why we've chosen to call our book *A Book of One's Own.*

(You probably should know that the printer originally missed the point of the book and called this "A Book of One Zone." But there are some problems you do get to fix, even when publishing the traditional way.)

CHAPTER 2

PUBLISHING

BASICS

Knowing how traditional publishing works will help guide your home-publishing project. Because most home-publishing projects involve most of the steps used in traditional publishing, this chapter will give a quick overview of the traditional publishing process.

Let's assume you have just come up with a brilliant idea for a new book: There are zillions of books on the market on managing your personal finances, but all from a similar viewpoint, so you decide to present the opposing viewpoint in *The Bozo's Guide to Financial Ruin*.

QUERY LETTERS AND PROPOSALS

The first step is to let people in the publishing industry know of your brainstorm by means of a query letter or a proposal. A query letter quickly outlines the story idea, your credentials, and the market for that idea — all in one page. Somewhat more elaborate is a proposal. Proposals usually run from 15 to 40 pages, and include five parts:

- cover letter
- chapter-by-chapter outline of the book
- analysis of competing books
- author bio
- sample chapter

For more information on proposals, see *Write the Perfect Book Proposal: 10 Proposals That Sold and Why* by Jeff Herman and Deborah M. Adams (New York: Wiley).

You send your query letter or proposal to agents or publishers — making sure you only approach those who are interested in personal finance titles. (The information on who handles what is available in the books listed on page 7 or go to the bookstore and see who is publishing books like yours.)

PRINTERS, PUBLISHERS, VANITY PRESSES, CONTRACT PUBLISHERS, AND PACKAGERS

Many people confuse publishers and printers, and get even more confused when you mention vanity presses, contract publishers, and packagers. Here is how to tell them apart:

- A *printer* prints books. If you take your publishing project to a printer, the printer will (for a fee) print up the number of copies you specify and deliver them to you.
- A *publisher*, as you might guess, publishes books. Publishers buy the rights to the book from the author (usually paying a *royalty*, which is an amount paid to the author for every copy sold); arrange to have the book edited, designed, and printed; advertise the book; and distribute it (which means getting it into bookstores, book clubs, and so on).

- A *vanity press* is sort of like a publisher, with one major difference: the author pays the publisher, rather than the publisher paying the author. If a publisher offers to publish your book for a fee, be careful. Vanity presses have a well-earned poor reputation, which they built by overcharging authors, printing shoddy books, printing very few copies, spending nothing on advertising or promotion, and having little or no ability to distribute the book.

- A *contract publisher* will also publish your book for you for a fee. Unlike vanity presses, contract publishers will specify the editing, design, and printing charges in advance, and will not normally offer to advertise the book or distribute it for you. A contract publisher might be a good choice if you really don't want to do it yourself. You can find them listed in the *Yellow Pages* under Publishers' Services.

- A *packager* prepares books for book publishers. The packager usually pays for the writing, editing, design, and printing. The publisher pays the packager a per-book rate for the books, and advertises and distributes them. Packagers usually come up with the book ideas and sell them to publishers, so packagers are unlikely to be interested in your book idea. It may, in certain circumstances, be possible to sell your book to a publisher as a package — which is how this book was produced. (See Chapter 12 for details.)

AGENTS

Agents serve two main functions for writers: they find publishers and they negotiate contracts. The typical agent works with the author to polish the proposal so that it is ready for submission to publishers, decides which publishers are most appropriate for the title, and sends it to the publishers. The agent then negotiates on the writer's behalf with any publisher who is interested in the book.

The agent often will sell the book to publishers in different countries, and in some cases also tries to sell the movie rights, software rights, or CD rights. The agent collects the money from the publisher and sends it to the author, keeping a portion (usually 15%) as a fee.

WHEN HOME PUBLISHERS NEED AGENTS

Home publishers usually don't deal with agents, but there are three cir-cumstances in which an agent can be useful:

1. Sales of your book have taken off! You really don't want to focus so much energy on mailing out 300 copies a week. It's time to bring in an agent to find a publisher or distributor for your proven winner.

2. You suspect your book will probably sell better in Britain than in Canada. An agent can help find a publisher or dis-tributor in another country.

3. A publisher or distributor has noticed your home-published book and has expressed interest in it. An agent can negoti-ate a distribution or publishing deal for you.

What the publisher buys from the writer is the right to publish the book under various conditions, which are specified in the contract between the publisher and the writer. The contract spells out such factors as when the author has to deliver a finished manuscript, which markets the books can be sold in, how much the writer will be paid, and what happens when the book goes out of print.

Typically, the writer still owns the copyright on the book. The publisher pays a royalty for the right to use that copyright. In some cases, the publisher will buy the copyright from the author for a specified amount.

COPYRIGHT

Copyright means exactly what it says: whoever owns the copyright on a publication has the sole right to make copies of it. If you own the copyright on material, no one else can use it in any form, whether print, electronic, or otherwise, without your permission. Likewise, you can not publish copyrighted material without the permission of the copyright holder. Copyright is usually, but not necessarily, held by the author of the work. If you want to reproduce copyrighted material in your own book, you should contact the publisher of the original work to obtain permission. Remember that copyright is not just for writing; it extends to design, illustration, and photographs as well. If your book will reproduce anyone else's work, you should ensure that you have the copyright holder's permission to reproduce it.

In Canada, you automatically hold copyright to anything you have written, and you do not need to renew that copyright. The copyright lasts for 51 years after you die. If you own the copyright to a publishable work, your will should specify who will inherit it should you die.

When the copyright expires, the work becomes "public domain," which means that anyone can reprint it without paying any fee to the copyright holder.

EDITORIAL

There is wide variation in how editorial departments in publishing houses are organized. Chapter 4 of this book examines the editorial function more closely. For the purposes of this quick overview, it is enough to note that the editorial department acquires, edits, and proofreads the book. In doing so, the editors usually deal with the production and sales department.

Since you're taking care of these functions yourself, your home-publishing project will demand that you ask the following questions about the manuscript:

- Who will offer an impartial evaluation of the book's organization and writing?
- Does it need a structural edit?
- Who will copyedit the book?
- Who will proofread the book?
- Does the book need an index?
- Who will arrange for an ISBN and for the CIP data? (see box on Editorial Legalities)

EDITORIAL LEGALITIES: Getting Your Book's
ISBN and CIP and Registering it with the National Library

The National Library of Canada keeps track of all the books published in the country. It assigns each publisher a list of ten-digit International Standard Book Numbers (ISBN). The ISBN of a book is its unique fingerprint, identifying a single publisher and publication, and is embedded in the bar code on the back of the book. No two books in the world are ever registered under the same ISBN (unless someone at the publishing house or filing office has made a terrific mistake!).

If you simply plan to distribute your print run to family and friends, you won't need an ISBN. However, if your hopes stretch farther afield and you want to make your self-published book available to the book trade (be it to bookstores, wholesalers, or libraries) you'll absolutely need to obtain an ISBN before you go to press. It's essential to the distribution, sales, and tracking process in the industry and your self-published work won't make it into bookstores without it.

The same application process applies whether you're a huge book publisher or only ever plan to sell a hundred books. The office will need the publisher's name, even if it's the same as yours, and a title. Happily, registering your book is free and can be completed in a matter of hours. You can get an application by calling the National Library's Cataloguing in Publication Office at (819) 994-6872.

After you've acquired an ISBN, you'll need to get its close cousin assigned to your book: the Cataloguing in Publication (CIP) data. The CIP data gets included on the copyright page on the back of the title page. While the ISBN only reveals a book's publisher, title, and language of publication (if you can crack the code), the CIP data is far more descriptive. A book's CIP information is very similar to what you would find in a library catalogue, including subject headings and classification numbers. When you apply for CIP data, the office creates a bibliographic record on a database that is linked to various bibliographic products, used by wholesalers, booksellers, and libraries around the world. What this means is that you may get a whole lot of unwanted phone calls if you're intending to market your book only to family members, so be forewarned.

You can request the CIP form at the same time as you get your ISBN application, but remember that you'll need the ISBN first. Because the CIP cataloguing process is more involved, allow two weeks for it to be completed. The central CIP office will tell you where to send the CIP form in your area.

Once your book has been published, send two copies to the Cataloguing in Publication Office for their archives, where they'll keep it for posterity.

PRODUCTION

The production department of a publishing company typically deals with budgets and schedules as well as design, layout, and printing. Obviously, these are all major areas of the publishing process, and each will be dealt with in depth later in this book.

Production is one of the main areas that derail home-publishing ventures. Desktop publishing software has made it very easy to prepare book pages very badly. Small local print shops have made it easy to print up bound sets of those badly designed pages very shoddily. One of the main goals of this book is to point out the major book-production pitfalls. Questions to ask yourself about production include:

- Should I use offset or digital or handmade?
- Who will design the cover?
- How many colours will appear on the cover?
- Who will design the pages?
- Will there be any use of colour, illustrations, or photographs inside the book?
- Who will lay out the pages?
- Who will print the book?
- How many copies should be printed?
- What paper stock should be used to print it?
- If the book is to be sold in stores, who will arrange for a barcode for the back of the book?

SALES AND MARKETING

The publishing house's sales department is involved right from the initial stages of the preparation of the book. In many publishing houses, sales people have a direct voice in deciding which titles will be published. They have input on the price, on the format, and even on the title.

They are responsible for preparing catalogues advertising the publisher's titles and for media advertising (often in conjunction with bookstores). Their publicists send out review copies and press releases, and arrange for author readings, interviews, and tours. They try to persuade bookstores to stock the book, to put the book into store windows, and even to display it in specially designed cardboard display cases.

If you are self-publishing, don't wait until your books are printed! You really should know the answers to the following questions before you finish the manuscript. You absolutely have to know the answers before the book is designed, because the answers to the questions will affect the design. Don't wait until you have cartons of books in your basement before you start thinking about:

- What price should the book sell for?
- How will it be advertised?
- Will it appear in a distributor's catalogue?
- Will it be sold through a distributor?
- Will it sell in bookstores?
- What discount will you offer bookstores that carry it?
- Will a freelance publicist be promoting you and the book?
- Will there be any attempt to get the book reviewed or to get you interviewed by the media?

DISTRIBUTION

It is the quintessential publishing nightmare: the book is wonderfully written and beautifully designed and printed; the major media have given it glowing reviews; the author has been interviewed on *Oprah* — and readers can't find copies of the book for sale anywhere. By the time the books reach the shelves a month later, those readers have forgotten all about it.

The distribution arm of the book publishing firm is responsible for warehousing the book and getting it to sales outlets as quickly and efficiently as possible. Distribution is the one publishing function that is toughest for the home publisher. The ideal home-publishing project doesn't call for wide distribution. It is easy enough to visit a dozen local sellers with a carload of your local history book every month or so. That's tougher to do nationwide!

If your book has the potential to reach a wide audience, your distribution should have the same potential. It is possible to arrange for a distribution firm to put the book in their catalogue, arrange to ship it to bookstores, and collect the revenue from the stores — but that is expensive. An easier way is to advertise it directly on the Internet and send out copies yourself. You'll find much more on distribution pitfalls and strategies in Chapter 12.

PUBLISHING IN A LARGER CONTEXT

Canadian publishing is just a small part of the huge worldwide publishing industry. International publishing operates by means of the sale of rights. A publisher in Germany, for example, might offer to buy the German-language rights to a Canadian title. These rights sales take place at book fairs. The largest of these are:

- the Frankfurt International Book Fair (October, Germany)
- the Bologna Children's Book Fair (April, Italy)
- BookExpo America (April/May, location varies)
- Guadalajara International Book Fair (November/December)
- London International Book Fair (March, London)
- Paris Book Fair (March)

If your title has potential sales outside of Canada, you should consider investigating foreign distributors and publishers. You're probably not going to be able to afford to flit from Paris and London in March to Bologna in April to sell the German rights to your book! (But it is a nice fantasy.) If your book is selling well in Canada, though, and you think it has international sales potential, there's a very friendly and helpful organization that is willing to flit on your behalf. It is called the Association for the Export of Canadian Books (AECB). For each major fair, AECB produces "rights catalogues" listing books for which Canadians are trying to sell the foreign rights. Home publishers are able to list their books in the rights catalogues — the catalogues are not restricted to traditional publishers. AECB can also provide "market intelligence." AECB explains how it works on its very helpful Web site at **http://aecb.org/Indexeng.html**.

The book publishing industry is a maze of associations, some of which can be very useful to the home publisher. The Editors' Association of Canada's web site has an especially helpful section on publishing associations at **http://www.web.net/eac-acr/web/assoc.htm**. (Inevitably, some of the association web addresses below will go out of date quite quickly. The EAC site will provide you with up-to-date links, and also has links to non-Canadian resources.)

Some associations that offer useful services to Canadian home publishers are:

- Alcuin Society (**http://www.slais.ubc.ca/ users/alcuin/**) is a Canadian organization for people with a broad range of interests concerning books and publishing, including the book arts of printing, binding, papermaking, calligraphy, and illustration.
- The Association of Canadian Publishers (ACP) represents over 130 Canadian-owned book publishers, with members from all provinces. ACP encourages the writing, publishing, distribution, and promotion of Canadian books. (**http://www2.publishers.ca/ acp/default.html**) (See also the Canadian Publishers' Council.)

- The Book and Periodical Council, the umbrella organization for associations involved in the writing and editing, publishing and manufacturing, distribution, and selling and lending of books in Canada, is the publishing industry's main lobbyist. **(http://www.interlog.com/~bkper/)**

- The Canadian Association of Photographers and Illustrators in Communications (CAPIC) maintains a database of CAPIC members by style and specialty. It is used to respond to enquiries from potential clients about book and magazine photographers and illustrators. **(http://www.capic.org/)**

- The Canadian Authors Association, which has branches nation-wide, offers meetings, workshops, and an annual conference to published and unpublished writers. CAA is an excellent resource if you need help polishing your writing. **(http://www.canauthors.org/)**

- The Canadian Booksellers' Association's annual trade show offers an excellent opportunity to promote your book to virtually every bookstore in the country. **(http://www.cbabook.org/)** See Chapter 12 for more information on this organization.

- The Canadian Publishers' Council (CPC) represents the interests of 30 companies who publish books and other media for elementary and secondary schools, colleges and universities, and professional reference, retail, and library markets. (Grossly simplified, the CPC represents the big publishers and the ACP represents the others.) **(http://www.pubcouncil.ca/)**

- The Editors' Association of Canada **(http://www.web.net/eac-acr/)**, with branches across the country, offers regional referral "hotlines" for people needing editorial help.

• The Graphic Designers of Canada's web site (**http://www.gdc.net/home.htm**) has links to the sites of many of the association's members, to help you find professional design help.

• The Indexing and Abstracting Society of Canada (**http://tornade.ere.umontreal.ca/~turner/iasc /home.html**) has a referral service for anyone needing a book index prepared.

• The Institute of Technical Editors (**http://ite.ca/**) will help you find a technical or scientific writer or editor.

• The Writers' Union of Canada (**http://www.swifty.com/twuc/**) is a national organization of professional writers of books for the general public. The Union maintains a list of reputable agents, mostly for the use of its own members, but also available to the general public.

The next chapter guides you through the two preliminary steps in most publishing projects: preparing a budget and a schedule.

CHAPTER 3

ANALYSIS NOT PARALYSIS

There are two essential elements to virtually every publishing project: a budget and a schedule. This chapter leads you through the process of preparing both of these.

THE BUDGET

Publishing projects have a way of costing more that you dreamed possible. This chapter will help you anticipate and control your costs. Of course, if you are producing a photo-copied, hand-bound book entirely by yourself, cost is not going to be a major consideration and you can skip this section. If you are independently wealthy, you can probably get by without a budget, too. (Of course, you didn't get to be independently wealthy by ignoring budget considerations!)

THE SCHEDULE

Do you need to produce your books by a certain date? If so, you need to prepare a schedule. Even if you have no "due date," you should have some idea of how long each step should take.

This chapter ends with a sample budget and schedule. But before we get to them, it is useful to consider the steps in the process individually, to look at how long they typically take and how they affect costs. The following estimate table shows what it would cost if you paid a professional to do each step and how long each step should take.

BUDGET AND SCHEDULE ESTIMATE

Step	Cost	Time	Comments
Prepare budget	nil	Varies	Don't get started publishing your book before you know what it will cost and how much revenue it will likely bring in.
Establish schedule	nil	Varies	The more hurried the schedule, the more things tend to cost.
Write first draft	30 cents per word	500 words per day	Most of the people reading this book have already written the manuscript. This discussion is just to put the work they've already done in context. Writing speeds vary widely. At 500 words a day, which is a rate that professional writers often quote, a 100,000-word manuscript takes 200 work days, or most of a year. And at 30 cents a word, the writer has earned $30,000 for that year's work. Writing is usually billed by the word, with rates ranging from about 20 cents a word to over $1 for corporate work and some magazine writing.

Step	Cost	Time	Comments
Obtain permissions	varies	varies	If you are printing something you didn't create, whether it is a portion of someone else's text or an illustration or photograph, you have to have the permission of the owner of the rights. Tracking down that owner and getting written permission can be extremely time-consuming. In many cases, you have to pay for the permission, which can become expensive very quickly.
Rewrite, if required	30 cents per word	500 words per day	Same comments as under writing. As a home publisher, you NEVER want to get into something as expensive as paying someone to rewrite your manuscript.
Edit for substance and structure	$20-$50 per hour	Varies from 100 to 1,500 words an hour.	Substantive editing is discussed in Chapter 4.
Edit for style	ditto	About 1,200 words an hour	Stylistic editing is discussed in Chapter 4.
Copyedit	ditto	About 1,500 words an hour	Copyediting is discussed in Chapter 4.
Title page, copyright page, cover copy,		One day	A whole batch of niggling little publishing chores that don't take long individually but can add up.
Index	$200 per 10,000 words is typical	10,000 words a day	See chapter 5 for a discussion of indexing. The time it takes to prepare the index depends on the complexity of the book and how detailed an index is required.
Design	$500-$2,000	1 week	Includes front and back covers and internal design.

Step	Cost	Time	Comments
Layout	$8-$25 per page	Varies considerably	When you are getting quotes on layout, find out how long it should take.
Illustrations	$30-$500 each	Varies considerably	Discussed in Chapter 5.
Proofread first pages	$20-$40 an hour	1,500 to 3,000 words an hour	The proofreader is responsible for checking the work of the copy-editor and the layout person, so how quickly a book can be proof-read depends on how thoroughly it was edited and whether a professional layout person was used.
Check second pages	ditto	3,000 to 5,000 words an hour	
Check final pages	ditto	A few hours	
Check printer's proofs	ditto	A few hours	This check is often done at the printer's premises. It is the final step, just before the printer is ready to start the presses rolling. Making changes at this stage is extremely expensive.
Printing, paper and binding	Varies widely	One day to six weeks.	The time it takes to print and bind a book depends largely on the printing and binding methods used, and the quantity to be printed.
Promotion and sales	Varies widely	Varies widely	See Chapter 12

A SAMPLE BUDGET

The following budget tries to make a slight profit on selling 300 of the 500 books in the initial print run. How realistic that sales target is really depends on the individual project. It is far better to set the projected sales as low as possible and get a pleasant surprise than to be too optimistic and lose a fortune. A good sales figure for your budget is 50% of your lowest projection.

TYPICAL SELF-PUBLISHING BUDGET:
a 128-page paperback with no interior illustrations

Expenses

Design	$300.00	A simple cover design and a prepackaged interior design template.
Editing	$900.00	Copyediting only.
Layout	$600.00	Following a very simple template.
Proofreading	$400.00	One proofreading pass; you check that the corrections were done properly.
Print 500 copies	$2,500.00	Printed offset; Cerlox bound
Contingency	$300.00	Some "just-in-case" money
Total Expenses	$5,000.00	
Cost per book	$10.00	"Real" publishers try to keep this figure down to 1/5th or even 1/7th of the selling price of the book. This fraction is called the "multiplier."

Income

Cover price	$29.95	You don't have as much control over the cover price as you'd like. It has to be pretty much in line with the price of similar books. This price is very high for a short paperback, but the project loses money at a lower price.

Less 40% discount	$17.97	The typical discount offered to book-stores by publishers is 40%.
Income from 300 sales	$5,391.00	Assumes the other 200 are returned by bookstores. This 40% return rate is, if anything, optimistic – some books have suffered much higher return rates than that.
Cost of sales @ $1/book	$300.00	Assumes you deliver most copies to bookstores in person.
Profit	$91.00	The good news is that this very low profit figure is based on a very low sales projection.

That budget looks pretty horrifying, right? All that work and expense to basically break even! Home publishing isn't normally about making pots of money. Most home-publishing projects are labours of love, with the goal to see something worthwhile in print, rather than to see a huge profit. With that in mind, most of the rest of this book points out ways to do these steps by yourself, so that you can avoid incurring unwanted expenses.

SAMPLE SCHEDULE

Most home-publishing ventures are done without any schedule in mind, which is as it should be. Most readers can skip straight to the beginning of Chapter 4. But if you need your book to be finished by a particular date such as the date of a fundraising event, read on!

Schedules are prepared by counting backwards from the delivery date. To make this really explicit, this sample schedule is presented "upside-down," with the end-date in the first line.

Step	How long the step takes	Target date for completion of that step
Target date to have books in bookstores		September 1
Delivery to stores	1 week	August 24
Printing and binding	1 month	July 24
Indexing	2 days	July 22
Proofreading and correcting	1 week	July 15
Layout	1 week	July 7
Incorporating editor's suggestions	1 month	June 7
Editing	2 weeks	May 24
Design	1 week	May 17
Writing	6 months	November 17 (previous year)
Start date	—	June 17 (previous year)

This schedule is fairly typical. Of course, a schedule like this is only necessary when you have a definite target completion date. Early September is the most common target date in book publishing, because books published in the early fall benefit the most from the Christmas buying season (but it also means your book is competing for attention with all the bestsellers).

CHAPTER 4

PREPARING THE MANUSCRIPT

You've finally taken care of the biggest hurdle of all: you've written the manuscript. (Why are we skipping over the writing process? Because there are literally tens of thousands of books out there on the subject, and because we know that a considerable proportion of the readers of this book have already written their manuscripts.)

Before you start preparing that literary-prize acceptance speech, be forewarned: as we have seen in that sample schedule, writing is only the first step in the long process of bringing a book to print.

This chapter explores the work that happens after the first draft is written: the notorious (and only sometimes painful) editing process.

PREPARING THE MANUSCRIPT

Book publishers expect manuscripts to be submitted in a specific format: single-sided, double spaced, 12-point type, and one-inch margins all around. There are various reasons for this. The standardized format (which has about 250 words a page) allows the publisher to estimate production costs very easily, and allows enough space for editorial corrections and comments.

Whether you as a self-publisher need to use that format depends on how the book will be produced. If it is going straight from your word processor to a desktop publisher, it really doesn't matter if you've strictly followed the format. If you intend to send it to a professional editor, the editor will probably be more comfortable working on the manuscript if it "looks right." Ask the editor; most editors are really put off by non-standard manuscripts, but some don't care.

When sending a manuscript to an editor or designer in the form of a computer file, the rule is really clear: "keep it simple." The editor or designer won't want lots of fancy fonts and pages that look like final layout. In most cases, they'll just have to undo the formatting before they start working on the file. So don't bother with the formatting unless the book is going to the printer right from your word-processed file.

HANDWRITTEN MANUSCRIPTS

At virtually every workshop for first-time writers and would-be home-publishers, someone asks: "Is it all right to submit handwritten manuscripts to publishers or editors or designers?" The answer is a resounding "no." There's not much that any of those people can do with a handwritten manuscript other than send it off to be keyed before they start working on it — and submitting something handwritten just looks extremely amateurish.

KNOWING WHEN TO STOP TINKERING WITH THE MANUSCRIPT

There's no rule on when enough is enough. To a large extent, you'll have to rely on your own instincts. If you feel that you need help, trust that instinct. If you find that you've changed large parts of the manuscript back to how they had been in a previous draft, and are still not comfortable with them, get someone to help. If you're struggling with writer's block, or know that there is a problem with the manuscript but can't quite explain what it is (or just plain never want to see it again!) stop tinkering and get a friend or editor to look it over.

How Can an Editor Help You?

Anyone at all familiar with the publishing process will tell you that a skilled editor does much more than correct spelling mistakes. An editor is an organizer who rereads, revises, rearranges, reevaluates, and in some cases, rewrites an author's book. The editor is there to polish the manuscript and make sure it's fit to print. If you can afford a professional editor, that's the way to go. But if you're on a budget, you'll want to consider self-editing.

FREELANCE EDITORS

Most publishing companies use professional freelance editors to edit their books. If you have the budget, a freelancer can take on a variety of editing chores for you. Freelancers have widely varying levels of ability and fee schedules. If you want to have your book edited professionally, get at least two quotes on the work and be sure to get (and check!) references. To find freelancers in your area, contact the Editors' Association of Canada (see Chapter 2 under "Publishing in a Larger Context" for EAC web site details), or look under "Editing" or "Publishing services" in your local *Yellow Pages*.

THE ART OF SELF-EDITING

Self-editing requires a great deal of objectivity and meticulousness (qualities that many otherwise detail-oriented people lack when confronted with their own writing). As a self-editor, you should be prepared to make many changes to your manuscript before you complete a final draft, from the broadly conceptual cutting and pasting of structural editing to the technical refinement of the copyedit. The following pages outline some basic components of each type of revision you will need to perform in order to make your self-published book the best it can be.

Keep in mind, however, that no one should be expected to write, edit, and publish a book completely alone. It's a good idea to get some input from a potential reader before the book goes to press. If you want to publish a book that is engaging and error-free, give it to a friend or colleague you trust and ask for some objective feedback. But beware: most people are reluctant to criticize. You'll often have to grill the reader to find out what was really wrong with the manuscript. If you find yourself in serious disagreement with a friend's comments, give it to someone else for a second opinion. Keep in mind that each person's sense about a piece of writing is subjective.

It's also important to remember that, when you ask a friend to read your work, you are requesting a favour. A surefire way to predispose people to dislike your work is to behave as though it were an honour that they should be "allowed" to read it.

What is Editing?

Editing includes making a manuscript logical, entertaining, clear, and consistent. It is an extended process, with several stages:

Rewriting. It is often easier to give a manuscript with major problems a total rewrite rather than try to polish it. The rewriter uses the manuscript as a source of ideas and information, but writes the book again from scratch. Rewriting is EXPENSIVE! It typically takes six months to rewrite a book, so you can expect to pay the rewriter the equivalent of six months' salary.

Substantive or structural editing. If the material is reasonably well written but poorly organized, repetitive, or incomplete, it needs a structural edit (also called a substantive edit). The editor reorganizes the manuscript, asking lots of questions and pointing out gaps in the logic.

Stylistic editing. The material is there and it is well organized, but the wording is clumsy, flat, or bureaucratic. A stylistic editor "translates" the manuscript, giving it the right words and tone.

Copyediting. What most people call "editing" is copyediting — fixing the grammar and spelling and watching for inconsistencies. This is also called "line editing."

Proofreading. A proofreader checks the work of the copyeditor and layout person. Many people mistakenly call the entire process "proofreading," but most proofreaders bridle at copyediting jobs disguised as proofreading. If it hasn't been copyedited, it isn't ready to be sent for proofreading!

For the self-editor, these stages will naturally overlap and merge as you embark on the path of revising your book. When looking for spelling errors, you will inevitably find yourself noticing organizational problems, and vice versa. Given this, the rest of this chapter is divided according to the basic principles at the heart of the editing process: rewriting, rearranging, stylistic editing, making the text correct and consistent, and checking. And as for the cherry on top? There's also advice on how to come up with a knockout title.

Rewriting: Almost Back to Square One

The manuscript just plain doesn't work, and you don't know where to start fixing it. You really need help with it — but can't afford to hire someone for the months it will take. Where do you turn?

Many freelance editors are willing to do a manuscript evaluation. They don't actually edit the manuscript. Rather, they read it through and prepare a detailed memo outlining what works and what doesn't. They also offer suggestions on how to fix the problems they've pointed out. You end up doing most of the work yourself, but you are doing it with professional guidance — and you've paid someone for a few days of work, not a few months. The Writers' Union also offers a manuscript evaluation

MAKING IT ENTERTAINING

Most manuscripts, whether fiction or nonfiction, need to entertain their readers in order to keep them interested. Fiction editors use a variety of "formulae" to make books entertaining. A formula is a standard "structure" — a way of organizing the information in the book. Here is one of the most common structures: You start with a fairly interesting incident to get the reader's attention, slowly build reader interest until the first climax, which comes about halfway through the book. That is followed by a section showing the consequences of the climax, with a slow, sustained buildup of tension until a more major climax at the end of the book. In other words, introduction> plot development> minor climax> more plot development> major climax> denouement. It works just as well for a family history as it does for a Harlequin though not a do it yourself.

service, as do the various writers in residence at universities, colleges, and libraries. (See also the Electronic Writers in Residence web page at **http://www.edu.yorku.ca/WIERhome/**.)

Rearranging: The Structural Edit

Not surprisingly, a structural edit involves reorganizing the book to make sure it progresses logically from start to finish. Rearranging can involve shifting entire episodes and sections around, or cutting the manuscript up into its constituent paragraphs and shuffling them into a more logical — or entertaining — order.

A few questions to ask yourself at this is point are: Do my thoughts follow in a logical order? Do I have all of the discussions of a single topic in the same place? Each of these factors will contribute to the clarity and effect of your work as a whole.

PUBLISHING WITHOUT POISONING: HOW TO CHECK YOUR COOKBOOK MANUSCRIPT

When publishing a cookbook, you want to make sure that your readers can follow your directions. If you can, test each recipe. Have a friend — preferably one who isn't a very good cook — try to follow the instructions. See where your friend stumbles or has to guess at your meaning and pay attention to the mistakes your friend makes. Be sure to taste the results, just in case! A good reference for cookbook editing is *Recipes into Type: A Handbook for Cookbook Writers* by Joan Whitman and Dolores Simon (New York: HarperCollins).

In terms of order, it's important to think of the assumptions and needs of your reader. For instance, if you are self-publishing an Italian cookbook, it's probably safe to assume that most readers will expect the text to proceed in a logical order: background and food information first, followed by antipasti, then entrees, then desserts. This is the order

---

in which most readers will normally consume a meal and the generally accepted order in which most cookbooks are written. But you should also consider other possibilities. What about organizing your recipes by region, or by menu? Either way, you should keep one thing in mind: a good structure is always one that makes your material more accessible to the readers you are trying to reach. As you reorganize, consider several different ways to present the same material. Choose the one that you think will be most useful to the reader.

Stylistic Editing

Paris Review: How much rewriting do you do?
Hemingway: It depends. I rewrote the ending to A Farewell To Arms, *the last page of it, thirty-nine times before I was satisfied.*
Paris Review: Was there some technical problem there? What had stumped you?
Hemingway: Getting the words right.

What Hemingway is calling rewriting is what we usually call stylistic editing. He's not rethinking and starting again from scratch — he is getting the words right. If you have all of the pieces of your puzzle in the right place, but the result still feels clumsy, it's time to "restyle." Restyling is a way to even out the textual bumps and potholes that may have been introduced during restructuring. Now's the time to add details to liven up particular episodes, add the explanations the reader needs to follow your argument, get rid of those sentences you wrote in the passive voice, or simply heighten the tension of a scene by adding in — or taking out — that perfect adjective. Rewriting also involves carefully going over each line of your book to make sure that your meaning is not being obscured by awkward language, confusing jargon, or clunky sentence structure.

But remember, the words you choose, and the order you place them in, constitute your own personal writing style. Stylistic editing is concerned with making a text more lively and readable, not more generic. During the self-editing process it is important to retain your particular, personal style.

~~MAKING THE TEXT SHORTER AND LESS VERBOSE~~

CONDENSING

Although it isn't unheard of for an author to underwrite, a far more common problem is overwriting. Extraneous details, trivial points, or out-of-place digressions distract the reader and obscure the point you are attempting to bring across. Overwriting, whether in terms of style or just sheer length, can usually be easily fixed by some strategic cutting and tightening within the text. This process is usually the most difficult part of the self-editing process. You must be objective enough to recognize when a word, sentence, or whole section of your book is unnecessary and extraneous.

Once the initial reduction work is complete, there are a number of questions self-editors must ask themselves upon re-reading their manuscripts, the most important of which is simply: Why? Why is this word/sentence/passage here? Why is it really necessary to the book as a whole? A careful editor must consider the worth of every paragraph, sentence, and word in relation to the whole.

The most important part of stylistic editing is establishing and maintaining the author's voice. To return to our Italian cookbook, if, in an early recipe, you communicate in a conversational, jocular voice ("My mother always taught me that sweet roasted peppers are tastiest if you slather on lots of good olive oil"), you should make sure that this mode of expression is consistent throughout the book. If you later instruct the reader in a more formal tone ("For best results, one must use liberal amounts of marscapone when constructing tiramisu"), you are using an inconsistent voice. Readers who have grown accustomed to your authorial voice will be jarred by any sudden shift in tone. This is your book, and your readers should be able to trust that it is the work of a single mind, unless, as in the case with this book, it is clearly presented as a collaboration.

RESTYLING YOUR CHILDREN'S BOOK

It is really difficult to write for children. Most children's book manuscripts fall into one extreme or another: they sound too adult, ignoring the child's reading level, or sound childish and patronizing. The best way to make sure that you will reach your audience is to do a field test. Have children of the appropriate age read the manuscript to you or read it to them. Encourage your reader to ask lots of questions. Pay particular attention to the places the child stumbles or starts to sound like a bureaucrat or a baby. Most of all, watch for places the child seems bored!

Copyediting

Being your own copyeditor means paying attention to the technical aspects of your manuscript, rather than to content. In essence, copyediting involves checking grammar, spelling, punctuation, and the general mechanics of style. At this stage you will also be checking for stylistic consistency within your book, as well as mapping out the placement of any graphics you are intending to use in the final product.

As your own copyeditor, you should make sure that the final text follows a uniform style. For instance, professional copyeditors will check that the text does not haphazardly jump from American to Canadian spelling. They'll also make sure that elements in the text have been given proper (and consistent) treatment: *italics* for foreign words (those memories of *la dolce vita* in your Italian cookbook) or **bold** for special emphasis (perhaps for **April 9, 1955** at the top of each diary entry in your journal). Copyeditors usually draw up a "style sheet" that will give them a blueprint reference for the book's style. Creating your own style sheet and following it from start to finish is a handy reference when preforming the copyedit. If you're wondering whether to write "25" or "twenty-five" (and can't remember if you were only spelling out numbers below ten or one hundred), it's much easier to consult a style sheet than to flip back through the book and see what you've done elsewhere.

BOOKS ON STYLE

Many books will guide you through the intricacies of making your book stylistically consistent. Which one you choose will depend on what kind of book you intend to publish. Academic publishers usually rely on the *Chicago Manual of Style* (Chicago: University of Chicago Press). Trade publishers often use *Words Into Type* (Englewood Cliffs: Prentice Hall). An easy-to-understand introduction is the New York Public Library Writer's Guide to Style and Usage (New York: Harper Collins).

Careful copyediting will give your self-published project the same professional, polished look as a conventionally published book. It's also a way to ensure that your book is free of embarrassing mistakes, such as typos, before it goes to press.

Proofreading

Once you think the book's pages are finished — copyedited and laid out (layout is described in the next chapter) perfectly — it is time to bring in a proofreader, and preferably one who has never seen the book before. The proofreader is the final safety net. A good proofreader will catch and correct mistakes made by everyone in the process, and will make the corrections in such a way that your cost and inconvenience are minimized. Don't even consider proofreading the book yourself. You are far too close to it, and will miss virtually everything that is wrong.

> ## SPELL CHEQUERS
>
> Don't rely on a spell checker on your word-processor to catch all of your spelling mistakes. Their real bad at caching allsorts of miss steaks — such as the properly spelt "wrong" words in the first part of this sentence.

If you are having a friend proofread the book, make sure that person has everything necessary for the job: the copyeditor's style sheet and the style guide and dictionary that were used. Point out the things that caused special grief ("We changed Laszlo's name to Pericles halfway through the process. Make sure there are no more references to Laszlo!").

Encourage the proofreader to ask lots of questions! Remember, this is the last person who is going to read the book all the way through before it is printed.

Finding a title

The last words you'll need to choose in the editorial process are the very first ones in the book: those that make up the title. Naming a book is not unlike naming a person — it needs to *feel* right, to fit the distinct personality of the work, and not just describe the contents. One need only imagine Salinger's *Catcher in the Rye* carrying the more literal title of *Holden Quits School,* or Shakespeare's *Twelfth Night* called *The Wonder Twins,* to realize the importance of choosing the right name for your book. Would Woody Allen's acclaimed comedy *Annie Hall* have seemed as funny under its cumbersome original title, *Anhedonia?*

Ideally, a title will perform several essential functions in the relationship between a reader and your text. Not only should it name the topic of your book, a good title should also indicate the tone (whether humorous or sober), the voice (whether formal or chatty), and the literary style of your project. If you are planning to market your book, remember that you will rely on the title as much as the design of your book to attract the curious eyes and hands of bookshop browsers. It may be a good idea to scan a few bookshops yourself and make a list of the titles your own eye is naturally attracted to.

It's a rare occurrence that a title reveals itself immediately. More often, an author uses a working title until a more catchy alternative jumps out of the text. It sometimes happens that the working title becomes a book's official title, but more often than not, a new title is required once the book is completely written and edited. A title should describe the contents of your book. That's the simple part. The hard part is choosing a name that, depending on the nature of your project, piques the interest of your intended reader. For instance, if your book is a family history aimed specifically at your personal family and friends, you'd be free to choose a title based on an inside family joke or reference. If, on the other hand, your book is meant to appeal to a wider audience, the book should correspondingly bear a more widely comprehensible title.

There are a number of techniques which will assist you in finding an engaging name for your work. One of the most tried and true ways of attracting a reader's attention is through the use of humour. A funny, resonant, or just generally effective title can emerge in countless ways, some of which include:

- alliteration: as with, *Boom, Bust and Echo* and *Sense and Sensibility*;

- word play on well-known titles: as with, *A Book of One's Own* and *The Joy of Sex*;
- purposefully long titles: as with, *In Grand Central Station I Sat Down and Wept* and *You'll Never Eat Lunch in This Town Again*;
- direct, topical titles: as with, *How to Advertise* and *How to Make Friends and Influence People*; or
- the setting or main character as the title of the book: as with *Howard's End* or *Jane Eyre*.

Once you've stumbled across the perfect title, it's time to start thinking about bringing your manuscript to print. The next chapter will outline the basic preparations you need to convert your manuscript into a legitimate book.

CHAPTER 5

TO
DESIGN A
BOOK

Your manuscript is complete. You are satisfied that the editorial process is quite finished. You now move on to the next stage in the production life of a book: its design. What is your goal as you prepare to design your book? Producing an object of beauty? Creating a unique look? Finally being able to use some of those delightful typefaces that beckon from your font menu?

Put all these thoughts aside, because your primary goal in designing your book must be to make it easy to read. If you design a book that is illegible, nothing you have written and no fancy printing job can salvage it.

Your second goal in your role as designer is to make the book look interesting. You can do this by infusing the pages with variety while working within a consistent framework. This goal goes hand-in-hand with ease of reading.

When you find a design that accomplishes both of these objectives, you will have successfully designed your book and perhaps, in the process, created a uniquely beautiful work that uses just one of those tempting typefaces!

> WHAT YOU NEED TO KNOW ABOUT DESIGN OF THE
> HANDWRITTEN OR TYPEWRITTEN BOOK
>
> Good book design is not restricted to those who use a computer; the
> principles apply to handwritten and typewritten books, too. Even
> though writing or typing your book limits many of your choices, this can
> be a benefit when you're just getting started, because it can help you to
> focus on the overall appearance of the book instead of the niggling
> details that prevent you from seeing the "big picture". Continue to read
> this chapter to appreciate the role and function of book design – along
> the way you'll learn lots about how to make any kind of book you pro-
> duce look and read better.

FINDING A BOOK DESIGNER

If you have the budget and you don't have an inclination toward design, or if your objective is to produce a lavish full-colour or hardcover book, you might want to hire a book designer. If this is the route you choose, you must look for a *book* designer. Any other kind of designer, whether they do print materials such as brochures, pamphlets, newspapers or catalogues, will not bring the book expertise that you need.

There are a number of ways to track down a book designer. Start with the design associations mentioned in Chapter 2, or you can look at an existing book for a design credit, and try to locate the designer. Just watch that the book you're looking at was produced in Canada; there's no sense in seeking a foreign supplier when many good designers are at work in this country. You can also check the reference book, *The Book Trade in Canada* (Toronto: Quill & Quire), in your local library; the Suppliers & Services chapter, Designers, Photographers & Production Services, provides some names. Finally, you can look under

Graphic Artists in your telephone directory. But, in this case, insist on someone with book experience, or it may be a case of the blind leading the blind.

Book designers charge a flat fee for their services; they are not paid a royalty. There will be one cost for the cover and one for the text. Just as printers need to know your printing plans, so too does the designer. Before they can even quote on a job, they need to know the number of colours in which the text and cover will be printed. In general, a cover design fee will range between $300 and $1,000; text will cost another $200 to $1,000.

At the low end of the range, you get one design. At the high end, a designer will usually produce three rough designs — but be sure about what is included by asking up front. If you reject these designs, you may face an additional fee for the designer to keep trying. More often than not, if the first three designs don't produce a look you like, there is a communication problem between you and the designer. It will help to describe your intended audience for the book, and if you have sensitivities to certain images, share this information with the designer.

Book design is an art, not a science. Be open-minded to new ideas the designer might bring forward, but don't sacrifice your vision either. After all, it's your book and your money, so get what you want.

MIX IT UP

Maybe your budget doesn't allow you to invest in a professional design-er to do both the cover and the text, but you can afford one part or the other. A cover is more difficult to design successfully than text, so buy that service and provide the design for the text yourself. You'll be rewarded with a very professional-looking book at less cost.

THE DESIGN PROCESS

Whether you are handwriting the pages of your book, typing them or preparing them in a computer program, there is a logical series of elements to consider in the design process:

1. the look of the book: its overall tone, style, size and shape;
2. type: words on the page;
3. pictures: art, in all its forms, on the page;
4. pages: the combining of the words and pictures to create the book pages.

THE LOOK OF THE BOOK

It makes sense to begin the design process by matching the tone of the contents with a corresponding design. Just as there are different styles of writing, so too there are different styles of design. If your book is a sober reflection on a serious subject, then plan for your design to be conservative and traditional. If you're publishing your memoirs and you're a vivacious person with many amusing anecdotes, your book should be friendly and playful in appearance. A children's book must be lively; a mystery shouldn't have loose ends.

At the end of this chapter you will find a Type Style Sheet which you can use to keep track of your design decisions. This will help you gather all the small choices into a cohesive whole when the time comes to begin making up pages. Your choice of style, then, will be your first entry on this form.

Also at the end of this chapter, you'll find another page where you can keep track of all your decisions regarding the elements of each page. Normally, we wouldn't encourage you to photocopy pages in a book, but for the Type Style Sheet and Page Style Sheet, we'll make an exception. Make at least one copy of each so you'll have a working copy and then a final for your file. Keep the originals in this book clean for future use!

Your next design consideration is to identify the reading audience for the book. The reading audience can be different from the intended audience: take a children's book that is meant to be read by a child. Its appearance will be quite different from a children's book that a parent will read to the child. Enter this information on the Type Style Sheet.

The overall style of the book is also determined by its size. A very distinct impression is made by a book that is very large, such as an art book, or very small, such as the tiny books often sold in stationers. Both are to be considered "precious," and you can see the extremes that publishers go to in order to create that impression!

Certain books are traditionally produced in certain sizes. It is unusual, for instance, to see a novel in an 8-1/2 x 11" size. Larger sizes, such as 8-1/2 x 11", are great for showing off illustrations, art and photographs, but they just aren't comfortable for people to hold for lengthy periods of reading. A minuscule book is a problem for the same reason: it's hard to read.

Therefore, if you are producing a book in which many photographs will appear, such as a family history, lean toward a larger size, such as 8-1/2 x 11". If you are producing an illustrated children's book, 8 x 8" or 8 x 10" is good, because the pictures will be shown to their best advantage. All other types of books can be designed in the range of 6 x 9" for a professional look.

The final consideration in selecting the size for your book depends on whether you plan to print the book pages off your laser printer for saddlestitched binding. Please see page 105.

Take time now to decide on a size for your book. Enter this information on the Type Style Sheet. If you have trouble deciding, go to your bookshelf. Look at the books you like and think about whether your book would be appropriate in such a size. When in doubt, it is better to err on the conservative side.

The shape of a book is another important design consideration. There are three usual shapes:

- vertical, also called portrait;
- horizontal, also called landscape;
- square.

Vertical: Most books have a vertical shape — taller than they are wide — when closed. It is an easy shape to work with, and to hold while reading.

Horizontal: This type of book is bound on the short edge to create a book that is wide instead of tall and is most customarily used for children's books.

Square: Even though both height and width are equal, square books are always bound on the left edge of the closed book. Square books are good choices for children's books and cookbooks.

If you are at all unsure of which shape you want, choose vertical. Include your choice on your Type Style Sheet. At this point the big picture is complete — you will see your book beginning to take form. Now it is time to move to the particulars and bring life to the page.

ASSEMBLING THE PIECES ON YOUR COMPUTER

All of the words are finally in place. It is all written and edited. Now its appearance has to be polished a bit before it is ready to face the public. How you do the polishing depends on how complex the document is, and how it is to be printed.

Use a word processor if:

1. the book is simple, without a lot of sidebars, boxes, footnotes, etc.;
2. the book has few or no illustrations, photographs, and so on;
3. the printer can work with word-processor files or laser-printed output.

Use a layout program, such as Quark or PageMaker, if:

1. the layout is complex;
2. the book is illustrated or uses colour;
3. the printer you choose asks for Quark or PageMaker files or EPS files or a printout that has printers' marks.

Mac or PC?

"Mac versus PC" has reached the point of being a religious question rather than a debate over the comparative merits of two computer systems. One of the authors of this book swears by PCs, the other is a Macophile. The book-publishing world is similarly divided. Editorial departments tend to use PCs; design departments tend to use Macs. For the most part, that is the result of the history of the development of the software available for the two operating systems. Macs for many years had no word processor that was as good as WordPerfect on a PC, and PCs couldn't match the design capabilities of Quark or PageMaker on a Mac.

We're not going to agree about which is best, but we do agree that either computer system is perfectly capable of turning out books of any complexity. Almost all of the software discussed in this book is available for both platforms. Use whichever system you find comfortable.

If you choose a PC, be very wary of taking your book to printing companies where the staff know only how to use Macs. Some printers will actually specify that files be delivered to them in a Mac format. If you use a Mac, follow the printer's instructions on formatting the Mac files. If you use a PC, there are plenty of PC-knowledgeable firms who will cause PC users far less grief than the Mac-only printers.

Word Processors

The market is dominated by two word-processing programs, Microsoft Word and Corel WordPerfect. Each is wonderful for relatively simple documents, and they each choke on complex documents. There are other word processors on the market, and some of these are very good at formatting text. The other word processors have such small market shares, alas, that it is difficult to find printers who can handle their files. So you can use your copy of XyWrite for your book if your printing company is going to work from laser-printed pages, but not if it has to work with the files.

Word and WordPerfect feel somewhat similar to use — they have similar user interfaces — but behind the scenes they operate in very different ways. In a WordPerfect file, the text is interspersed with formatting codes (some of which you can see using the Reveal Codes function). In a Word file, the text is all together near the beginning of the file, and the formatting instructions are all clumped together afterwards, with bookmarks specifying which text is affected by which formats. Some people argue that WordPerfect's file format is more stable when working with book-length documents. In truth, both behave badly with long or complex documents.

WordPerfect is more flexible and capable than Word when handling tables and multi-column pages.

Word and WordPerfect use similar processes for designing book pages. In both programs, you develop a template for your page layout grid, using different style tags for the different elements in the document. The style tags specify such things as font, margins, indent, spacing and other formatting factors. You then apply the template to your manuscript by going through the file and "tagging" each paragraph with the appropriate style.

That, at least, is how the programmers intend people to use both programs. Many users don't use templates and style tagging, instead manually formatting the text as they go. That works well enough for short documents, but is a disastrous strategy for long documents. This is because, if you've formatted the document manually, you have to go through the entire document, tweaking the layout every time you change a design element. If you've used a template, changing a style in one place changes it throughout the document, so that the document maintains a consistent, professional feel. If you intend to prepare your finished pages using a word processor, take the time to learn how to use templates and styles before you start.

A number of web sites have libraries of free Word and WordPerfect templates. Unfortunately, very few of those templates are useful for designing book pages, simply because the programs are so rarely used for book design.

Layout Programs

Layout programs offer far more control over the appearance of the book page than do word processors. They are also far more stable when working on complex designs or illustrations. For most book-publishing projects, it makes sense to use one of the major layout packages, which are available in PC or Mac formats.

There are four main page layout programs on the market designed for use with books. The following table is a very quick summary of the strengths and weaknesses of each.

PROGRAM	STRENGTHS	WEAKNESSES
Quark	• Excellent support for graphics	• Poor handling of long documents
PageMaker	• Better for long documents than Quark • Relatively easy to learn	• Can have problems with graphics and complex layouts
Ventura Publisher	• Relatively easy to learn, especially if you are familiar with WordPerfect • Good with long documents	• Few printers are used to dealing with Ventura files • Has a reputation for being buggy
Framemaker	• Excellent at book-length documents • Designed for use in academic publishing, so strong support of tables, footnotes, etc.	• Very difficult to learn • Few printers are used to dealing with Framemaker files

Quark, Pagemaker, and Framemaker are very expensive — about $1,000 each. Ventura is considerably cheaper.

Perhaps surprisingly, the layout programs use a concept that is rather similar to the "templates" found in word processors. They use "master pages". The design elements on the master pages, which you set up when you start, carry over to the individual book pages.

Illustration Programs

There are many illustration programs. The most widely used are Illustrator, Freehand and Corel Draw. What they have in common is complexity: all of them are very difficult to use competently, and unless you are very familiar with one of them we would very strongly advise you to get a professional illustrator to prepare any computer-generated graphics for you.

Scanning and Photo Programs

Scanning art, photographs and documents such as birth certificates is now very simple. Scanners come with software that will convert the scans into any of the common file formats. The usual problem with learning to scan is that beginners tend to use an unnecessarily high resolution and too large an image, so that the scanned files are gargantuan. Ask your printer what resolution to supply the scans. If it's high resolution scans you need for printing, you can make one set of low resolution scans for placing in your document and one set of high res scans on a separate disk which you supply to the printer for placing in the files. This keeps your working file at a manageable memory size.

Although Photoshop (which can be a challenge to learn) is the most popular imaging program among professionals, such less-complex programs as Microsoft Photo Editor (part of Microsoft Office) and Corel Photo House (part of WordPerfect Office) are much easier to use. Photo House is extremely easy to use and will probably meet all of your needs. Photo Editor, although possibly a bit trickier, is still very simple and gives you more image-editing options.

DESKTOP PUBLISHING?

Desktop publishing was originally defined as using a PC or Mac operating system to create type and make-up pages instead of typesetting with specialized typesetting equipment. Now, virtually all type is created on screen (the desktop) and the term "desktop publishing" is used to describe a rather unprofessional-looking finished book. Obviously, after reading this book, your book will never suffer this fate!

PHYSICAL MANIPULATION, OR HOW DO I GET THERE FROM HERE?

You've planned your pages and you're ready to put the art or photos in place. How will you move from originals to copies?

If you are planning to print all the pages from your computer off your printer, you must capture the images electronically, either by scanning the art with your own scanner or having it scanned elsewhere. Scanning services are provided by a variety of suppliers. Try your local photocopy shop first, or where you'd take your film to be developed. More sophisticated sources would be found under Graphic Designers in the telephone directory.

You will then import the scan into your pages. If you are printing in black ink only, then the pages can be printed from your printer in the quantity you need for binding, or as a single copy ready for xerography. To go on press, you will need to prepare an electronic file.

If your art is in colour, but the text is black only, and you have access to a colour printer, you can print out your colour pages and manually insert them into the text pages. If you do not have a colour printer, you can put your colour work on a floppy disk or other medium, and take it to a photocopy shop where it can be copied in colour.

Be forewarned that colour scans can eat up huge amounts of space wherever you park them — on the hard drive of your computer or the other electronic storage mediums. It is quite likely that the file size for a single photo will be too large for a floppy disk, so you will have to go the Zip, Syquest or CD route. Once you get into this kind of work, you are probably considering digital or offset printing. If so, explain to the printer's sales rep what you are doing and let the rep point out the ways the company can help you.

The problem here is that you will have produced an "insert" page that will not have text on the reverse. This is not very professional looking. The answer to this is called "tipping-in". To do this successfully, your colour piece should be smaller in dimensions than your page size. When the colour page is reproduced, there will be a white margin around the colour. Trim this off completely, and then apply two small dots of glue, such as rubber cement, to the wrong side of the two top corners of the art. Now position your colour art on the page. In effect, the book paper creates a frame around the art. This process can only be done after the pages have all been reproduced.

If you use high quality photo-grade paper, such as Polaroid Inkjet Photo Paper or Epson paper, to print the colour art or photos, you will have an excellent reproduction that can contribute enormously to the appearance of the book. You will, however, be producing each page from your printer, which could be a time-consuming process.

If you are not using a computer, take the originals to a copy shop where they can be photocopied and, in the process, enlarged or reduced. You will want one complete set of these copies made from all your originals. Then you can paste them onto your pages before they are once more either photocopied or actually printed. Unfortunately, quality will be sacrificed but this is still an inexpensive way of reproducing colour images.

TYPE

You could spend years studying the art of typography. It's a complete world, filled with its own language of ascenders, descenders, baselines and x-heights. But you don't need to know this language to choose the type form that is best for your book. What you do need to know is enough to get by to make a good set of decisions about type. Then you must exercise the discipline to carry those choices consistently through the entire book.

The Language of Type

A typeface refers to an entire family of letters of a design. Some well-known examples are Times Roman, Helvetica and Palatino. This book is set in Bembo.

There are 5 styles of type:

1. serif: lines project from each letter form: **T**
2. sans serif: sans means without; thus, without lines: **T**
3. script: letter forms simulate handwriting: *𝒯*
4. decorative: letter forms are given a special treatment: *𝒯*
5. special characters and symbols: special characters are created by a combination of key strokes. These characters create copyright, register and trade marks; currency symbols and accents. Symbols, also called dingbats, wingdings or dingthings, do not produce letter forms but a combination of numbers and/or symbols. Musical notation is one example of a symbol face.

When selecting a typeface, don't be conned by those artistic "interesting" type styles. Stick to a serif face for the body text — they've been around forever because they are easy to read and beautiful as well. Look at which serif faces are available to you; choose one and insert this on your Type Style Sheet.

If you have chapter openings and/or subheads within the text, you can use an alternate form of the body text type or one that provides contrast. Please see the chart on the following page for some suggestions; once you've found a good candidate, include that on your Type Style Sheet too.

PICAS, POINTS, INCHES OR CENTIMETRES?

Typesetting has traditionally used picas and points as units of measurement, such as the example given for type size. Except for describing type size in points, we will use inches and centimetres as our unit of measurement on the basis that everyone has a ruler in these everyday measures. Rulers with picas and points are available through art supply shops.

Now more decisions await you regarding the typeface you've selected. Each of the following elements needs to be defined on your Type Style Sheet. Some of the entries on this form have been completed for you because sometimes there are simply no options but the normal, especially when dealing with body type.

Type size and leading: Size is the vertical measurement of a letter. Leading is the space between lines of type. Both elements are usually measured in points, i.e. 12/16 pt expresses type that is 12 pts in height with 16 pts of leading. Leading is usually described in word-processing programs as being a single line space, 1.5 line spaces or double line spaces.

Weight: The density of the letters can be anywhere from light to extra bold.

Width: The horizontal measurement of a letter is described as condensed, normal or expanded.

Slant: The angle of a letter encompasses both roman (vertical) and italic (oblique) forms.

Style: The options applied to type include underlining, strikethrough, superscript, subscript, shadow, reverse and outline.

Case: Letters can be capitalized in different ways. They can be either upper and lower case, small caps or uppercase (all caps).

The Conventions of Type

To the amateur typesetter there can seem to be an almost overwhelming number of choices to make about type. Luckily there are certain rules that can make the process a lot easier:

- Don't ever use a type size for body text that is smaller than 10 pts (what you would customarily see in a business letter) or larger than 16 pts (an extra large children's fairy tale book, for instance).

- Don't scrimp on leading, but don't go overboard either. Generous leading invites legibility, but too much can look silly. Strike a balance between too little and too much. Usually 10 pt type is well balanced by 12 pt leading, 12 pt type with 14 pt leading, 14 pt type with 16 leading and 16 pt type with 18 leading.
- Make the line length proportional to the page size and dimension. If you are producing a book that is horizontal in shape, it can support longer lines. The longer the line, the larger the type. A line length should never exceed 5", and closer to 4" is optimal. Maintain wide margins all around.
- Use roman face for text.
- Use **bold** face to create emphasis.
- Use *italic* face for captions and quotes that repeat text from other sources.
- Use ALL CAPS for short "headlines" such as chapter titles; otherwise do not use all caps as a type treatment.

FORMATTING TIPS

Proper formatting of the text will produce a professional-looking book. Here are some tips that will make a big difference in the look of your book.

1. Insert only one space after punctuation: the good old double space at the end of a sentence is not used in typography.
2. Create proper dashes: instead of two or three hyphens, use an en-dash (–) or an em-dash (—).
   En-dashes are created by:
   Mac: space option hyphen space
   PC: ctrl =

Em-dashes are created by:

    Mac: option shift hyphen

    PC (WordPerfect): hyphen hyphen hyphen space

    PC (Word): hold down the ctrl, alt, and numlock keys and press the minus sign in the number pad

3. Create true quotation marks by:

Double quotes:	Mac: option [to open
	option shift [to close
	PC: Select the SmartQuotes option and quotes will be styled automatically
Single quotes:	Mac: option] to open
	option shift] to close
	PC: Select the SmartQuotes option and quotes will be styled automatically

4. Paragraphs that follow a head are called lead paragraphs. Don't indent them.

To make these changes throughout your manuscript, use the find-and-replace option for the double spaces, hyphens and quotes. Lead paragraph indents will have to be manually removed.

TYPE IN COLOUR

Why do you want type in colour? To create interest? Make the book look snazzy? To impress your friends?

Unless you are going to make the type all one colour instead of black, give it up! If any of the above reasons are your objective, go back and revisit your type specs, or (dare we say it?) your content. Type in colour is best left to the gifted typographic artists and the pros.

If you are looking for one colour other than black, it must have enough tone to provide sufficient contrast with the paper or the words will be lost on the page. So, you can use a dark-toned blue, brown or green, but given the fidgeting required to successfully pull it off, it's just not recommended.

WHAT MAKES A BOOK

There are three basic sections to a book. They are the preliminary pages, body and end matter. Not all books have end matter, and some are very light in the prelims; but they all have a body.

PRELIMINARY PAGES

The prelims include the half-title (if you are using one), title, copyright, contents, acknowledgments and foreword. These pages will be created singly and therefore designed individually.

While you must obviously work within the parameters of your page, there are no hard and fast rules for the design and make up of these pages. Let aesthetics be your guide, and design them to please the eye. Use common sense and remember your design objectives of legibility and interest.

Create a separate file for this portion of the book. When you have made a first pass to capture the information, save the file and back it up.

What goes where:

Half-title. If you are putting in a half-title, it will be the very first page in the book. This page is not necessary. The only type on the half-title is the title of the book. Quite often, the book title will appear in the same face as it does on the front cover, though it is usually smaller.

The back of the half-title is blank.

Title. The title page includes the title, subtitle, author's name and name and logo of the publisher. As with the half-title, the title and subtitle are often adapted from the front cover.

The back of the title page is the copyright page.

Copyright page. The copyright page contains all the legal stuff: copyright notice, rights notice, name and address of publisher, ISBN number and the library catalogue notice (CIP). In setting this page, you may find you have a lot to fit in a relatively small space. This is one of two places in the book where you may have to make your type size considerably smaller than elsewhere; the other is the index. Also, if you set this type smaller, this page will become less conspicuous than it otherwise might be.

The next page is usually the *table of contents.* If it is longer than one page, it will run onto the back of that page. Otherwise the back will be a blank. You will not be able to insert your page numbers on the contents page until the book is finalized. Follow convention in the creation of these pages. They are really just a buildup to the main event: page one!

PAGE 1 OR PAGE i?

Usually if the preliminary pages are numbered, roman numerals are used. Then the first text page is page 1. However, sometimes the very first page in the book is treated as page 1. The latter treatment makes it look as if there are more pages in the book, and helps to justify those high prices!

PAGE ONE AND ON: THE TEXT

This is what you've been waiting for: the chance to make a book starting with the first words of your manuscript.

The easiest way to create pages is to develop a grid. A grid is simply a structure for the type that is applied consistently across the pages. The beauty of using a grid is that many of your decisions regarding page composition are made once: when you design the grid. Without a grid, each page could be a nightmarish trial-and-error process and the book a mishmash.

A grid for book pages is different from other printed materials in that the type on a book page is usually formed in one wide column. Newspapers, magazines, newsletters and, occasionally, books that are wider than they are high, are formatted into multi-column grids. The longer line length of type on a book page brings a different set of design requirements than do other print materials.

The text pages are composed of the body (the story, if you will), with a running head that usually gives the title of the book on the left page and the chapter title on the right, and a page number (also called a folio) with each of them. When a new chapter begins, there is usually some combination of chapter number and name.

QUITE EXCEPTIONAL!

Of course, just as one establishes a set of rules or guidelines to try to simplify the book-making process, the exceptions start popping up. Bear these tips in mind for the most professional look in page design:

- Chapter openings don't have running heads.
- Children's books of less than 32 pages usually don't have page numbers.
- Picture pages on which a single image is featured don't need page numbers or running heads; sometimes, for the biggest impact, even the caption is placed on the facing text page.
- Preliminary pages usually don't have page numbers or running heads.
- End matter pages (bibliographies, indexes, etc.) usually have page numbers and running heads.

Just as you had to make decisions regarding the type itself, so too you must decide how and where to put the type within the grid. This is called alignment. Alignment describes how lines of type align on the page: left margin type aligns on the left margin, justified type aligns on both margins, centred type lines up down the centre of the page and right margin type lines up on the right margin.

Although most books have justified type, trying to justify the text can become a nightmare if you are using a word processor. You can end up with large spaces between words or even letters. If this happens, it is best to abandon justification and line up the text on the left margin.

Good applications for the alignment options are listed below:

Left margin: all books such as family histories, journals, memoirs, children's stories, novels, poetry, recipes or self-help

Centred: poetry or recipes

Right margin: captions that appear beside photos, art or other illustrative elements

You can also use different forms of alignment for different elements within a book. A cookbook, for instance, might have the recipe title and ingredients list set in a centred format, but the cooking instructions would be set starting on the left margin of the page.

GRIDS

There are three kinds of grids, but only two that are recommended for the home publisher: either the minimum or the simple grid. The professional grid is discussed briefly, but its execution requires a grasp of so many variables that its use is better left to the design experts.

The Minimum Grid

This grid is used for books that don't have page numbers, running heads, or, usually, chapter titles. It only delineates margins indicating where the story should be placed on the page.

The Simple Grid

The most simple grid doesn't distinguish between left- and right-hand pages. This means:

- equal margins on the left and right
- page numbers, chapter opening titles and running heads that are centred

Such a grid can be used for any kind of book. It is easy to work with and can be easily and quickly set up on your word processor. This grid is best for books of 60 or fewer pages in length; longer books will tend to look tedious. For a longer book, monotony can be avoided by introducing levels of subheads in the text in order to break up large text blocks; or using art — either illustrations, photographs, or technical art such as maps, charts and diagrams; and/or by using a second colour for some of the type.

The Professional Grid

This kind of grid is the trickiest to work with because the left- and right-hand pages are treated differently:

- The margin may or may not be equal on each side of the page.
- Page numbers and running heads are positioned on the left- or right-hand margins.
- The text type is usually justified.
- Chapter opening titles can be centred or not.

There's a lot of information to plan and track as the pages are assembled. To avoid frustration, this kind of grid should only be attempted after one of the easier grids has been used.

Making a Grid

You will have two options when it comes to making a grid: you can make your own, or you can use or adapt one of the grids you'll find in the Appendix, starting on page 177.

To make your own grid, you must enter all your decisions about how the pages will be formatted onto the Page Style Sheet, which is provided on pages 78 and 79. Just as the Type Style Sheet is your record of type decisions, the Page Style Sheet is how you will remember what you decided about how the pages will look.

When you have made all the necessary choices, it is a good idea to make yourself a "dummy" page:

- cut a piece of paper the size of the finished book
- pencil in the box where the text type will appear on the page
- draw a line to represent the running head and a capital X for the page number
- if there will be photos, draw a box to represent where the photo will be placed on the page, and lines to show the caption (if using)

Now, take a good hard look at what you've designed. Is there lots of space for the margins and between the type elements? Does it look like these pages are going to be easy to read? If not, keep trying by looking at other books until you arrive at a design that works.

The other way of developing a grid is to use one that is provided in the following pages. Even if you want to work up your own, seeing how the professionals do it will give you ideas and direction.

Once you're satisfied with your grid, set the parameters for margins, alignment, page numbers and running heads (also called headers) in your computer file in which you are making the pages. Then you must resolve to stick with it no matter how tempted you are to make exceptions!

END MATTER

End matter consists of the index, bibliography or other aspects of the book that are rightly placed at its end. If you have many pages that classify as end matter, you will want to create a grid; otherwise, if there is only a page or two, a grid is not required. Use good design sense to make sure the pages are legible and maintain the same margins as in the text pages.

PICTURES ON THE PAGE

If you plan to include any kind of pictures in your book, this section is for you. If you're not, skip ahead to the details on making up pages, page 71.

A wide variety of illustrations appear in books. There are photographs, art, documents (such as birth certificates, marriage licenses) and maps, lists, tables and graphs. We'll use the words "photos" or "art" to mean any illustrative element.

While books that include illustrations always look more interesting than those without, this interest is created and sustained only if the art meets certain requirements. The publisher should ask the following questions when selecting art for inclusion:

Does the art match the style of the book?

Just as you match type to the tone of the book, so, too, must illustrations be a good fit. Cartoons would be great in a kid's book, but they'll probably make a joke of that family history.

Can I change the tone of the book with art?

Yes, if you're very careful. Editorial cartoons, for instance, address very serious subjects using a lighthearted approach. You can try the same technique of using cartoons to enliven a self-help book, for instance. But be sensitive and err on the side of caution. Don't forget to ask for and receive permission from the artist or publisher before using art that appears elsewhere.

Is the piece of art technically sound?

Photographs must be in focus. They also need sufficient contrast to be easily discernible. Photographs of people must be at close enough range to see the faces.

Documents, charts and other technical art should be chosen with legibility in mind.

Is the artwork aesthetically sound?

Children's drawings can be charmingly naive, but will they appear so to anyone but the parents of the artist? Take a tough stand on this, even if you are the parent.

Photographs that are "negative" in mood or content tend to create a very negative reaction in the viewer. Many people feel that a photograph of something that's ugly can be really instructive, because they think it can show you what not to do. Forget about taking that approach. Show the very best — or the most beautiful — picture you can to make your point.

CLIP ART AND STOCK PHOTOS

Clip art is illustrations, usually in the form of line drawings, that come for use on the computer or in catalogues, where it can be "clipped" for use. There is a vast variety in colour and black only: some of it is great, some not so.

For instance, this illustration comes from DeskGallery Clip Art. It has been copied and pasted onto this page. Its size, colour and position can be adjusted on the page by editing the illustration.

The wonderful thing about clip art is the cost. It's free! Once you buy the original — on disk or CD or from a book— it's yours.

Stock photos are collections of photography compiled by agencies that specialize in this work. Again, the number and type of photos available is enormous and can be selected from catalogues on CDs, in books or on the Internet (see **www.digitalstock.com**). Common categories of photos include health and fitness, lifestyles, people, sports, business and industry, miscellany, nature, travel and wildlife. There is a cost for using stock photography, but the cost is much lower than if you hired a photographer to take the photograph for you.

Does the art correlate with and contribute to the text?

If the art — whether it's a photo, drawing, or chart — has no bearing on the text, it shouldn't be included.

Is it in good taste?

No, you can't be the arbiter of tastefulness to one and all. But if the photo or art in question will cause embarrassment to others, or if it qualifies as being questionable, do yourself a favour and keep it in your private collection.

Is it kind?

This is not a technique issue, but one to bear in mind in any case. By way of example let's say your child has produced an amazing portrait of her grandmother that shows a lovely smile, twinkling blue eyes, silvery gray hair — and the large wart on the side of her nose. Must you really preserve this for posterity? The same goes for photographs: if you have a choice, try for the flattering view.

WHERE TO PUT THE PICTURES ON THE PAGES

Pictures can be placed on the same pages on which text appears, on their own page, or in sections, to create the feel of a "photo album."

On the Page

If a photo and text are to be integrated on the same page, then the best — and easiest to manage — position for the photo is at the bottom of the page. In this case, the space the photo occupies on the page simply replaces space the text would have used. The photo does not go into the margin. However, this can quickly become rather tedious-looking. A good way to alleviate this problem is to occasionally insert full-page photo pages. The page facing the chapter opening is a good place to do this.

Photos on Their Own

In this case, the photo will be on its own on the page. This is how single images such as illustrations in a children's book are nicely accommodated. When a photo or piece of art is treated this way, it should be confined within a wide margin or "bleed" right off the page (see page 132 for a discussion about bleed). Each photo should be the same size on the page.

Photo Sections

Sometimes photos comprise their own section in a book and create the feel of a photo album. Multiple images, in different shapes and sizes, can be incorporated to be visually appealing. Such sections are usually not less than four pages each within the book; there may be any number of such sections.

Captions

Captions need to accompany almost all photos, documents and other art forms. Illustrations in children's books are the big exception. If at all possible, the caption should be informative, and not just repeat facts in the text. For instance, instead of simply stating the name of the person in a portrait, you could add a tidbit filling in details about the person. So "Lyla Buttle" would become "Lyla Buttle, founder of the mining community of Hailey's Station."

The type for captions should be one size smaller than the body text, and the leading should be tighter. An italic typeface is a handsome choice.

THE METHOD FOR MAKE UP

With your grid in place, you can then proceed to "make up" pages. This is also known as layout. It is a methodical process that requires patience; don't try to take shortcuts! Do things properly at this stage and you'll avoid future headaches.

Depending on what program you are using you will either import or cut and paste the text onto the grid page(s) you've created. If you keep the book in one file, the computer keeps track of which pages fall on the left and which fall on the right; the disadvantage is that you might have quite a large file to work with.

If you're not using a computer, you'll still want to follow the grid you've developed to ensure consistency across all the book pages. Take the paper that will become your book pages and lightly mark on each piece the guidelines you'll need to follow to place your text correctly. Faint pencil marks can always be erased later. Then, either write your manuscript in the text block space or cut and paste typewritten pages to fit within the guidelines.

Start page one on a right hand page and then let the text flow from there. Make sure you start new chapters on a new page but otherwise don't worry about fiddling with awkward word and line breaks; you want to get all the manuscript moved onto grid pages before starting the fancy stuff.

Once you've got this step accomplished, make a backup of your file on a floppy disk, CD, or some external means such as an FTP site.

Then go back to page one and start to apply your type styles. Apply each type style according to the decisions you made on your Type Style Sheet. Use your program's "Style" function. If necessary, learn how to use this to create the typography you have designed.

Make sure that you have tested your chosen typefaces before running through the entire book. Some fonts appear on the computer screen only and will not print. A quick check to make sure everything works, and looks, the way it is supposed to can save a lot of time.

Work on every page and every element of each page in sequence: don't jump back and forth. Treat chapter openings as you come upon them and deal with any "exceptions" as they arise. When you've finished, back this up.

This is now a good time to print out all the pages on paper. You will be surprised at the number of mistakes, inconsistencies, typos and omissions that will jump out at you from the paper that you just couldn't see on the computer screen. Read the pages carefully, and be sure that you're happy with the look you've created. It's not too late to go back in and make changes, but make sure you understand your rationale for such change. When this line-by-line, page-by-page review is completed, go back to page one in your layout and work your way through the book, fixing all the problems you've identified.

There will be two problems that you are certain to see when you look at these pages: poor hyphenation and what are called "widows" and "orphans".

Hyphenation. When a word fails to hyphenate, you can have a very large space on the end of a line. Such spaces disrupt the flow of reading and look ugly. Use your program's hyphenation function. You may also find words that have failed to hyphenate correctly; these must be fixed manually. If you're in doubt as to the correct way to hyphenate a word, use your dictionary. Finally some words may hyphenate correctly, but their hyphenated form is unconventional. For instance a line beginning with "ly" just looks bad. These, too, should be fixed.

Never begin a line with a dash or hyphen; if either starts on the left margin, force it onto the end of the line above or bring down a word to precede it.

Widows/orphans. Sometimes you will see at the top of a page the last line or two, or even just a few words, of the preceding paragraph. These lines or words look lonely, and in fact that's exactly how they are corrected: by giving them some company. If you need to add lines on a left-hand page, decrease the number of lines on the preceding two pages by one each and add these two lines to your widow. If you need to add lines on a right-hand page, decrease the number of lines on the page before and the preceding two pages by one each and add these three lines to your widow. If it's just a word or two, see if you can force it back onto the preceding page by some judicious editing. If this isn't possible, force lines to come forward. Most programs do this automatically.

It is quite possible in fixing some problems to create others. As you make changes, keep an eye out for what is happening to the lines above and below where you're working. Scan each page before going to the next. Finally, back it up and print it out again. This is your final check. At this point you'll have page numbers in place. This allows you to go back and complete your table of contents to finish up the preliminary pages, and to write your index.

WRITING AN INDEX

An index is essential in all non-fiction works for one good reason: it lets people find information easily and without guesswork. Computer word-processing programs with a sort function have made the creation of proper-name indexes a breeze. The best source of information about how to write the index is found in *The Chicago Manual of Style* (Chicago: University of Chicago Press).

If you're going to press with the book, when the pages are finished to your satisfaction, you'll need to provide your printing company with the materials from which they will make the film that produces the printing plates. If you're providing everything on disk, make sure it's in a format they can use. It's a good idea to make a small sample disk before the project is completed to ensure compatibility between your system and theirs. Always include a paper-copy print-out of the text. It is an important reference for the person who will do the manipulation of the files.

If you're providing the pages on paper, called camera-ready art, each page will need to be printed on the highest quality white stock. If photographs or illustrations form part of the book, each one will have to be identified as to where it goes, as well as its size. A photograph that is to be printed in its original size would be indicated to print, — this is called "sized at" — 100%; a picture that is to be half as large as the original you're supplying would be sized at 50%; twice as large would be 200% and so on.

If any of these steps cause difficulty for you, ask the printer of the job for help. Communication with the pros can save you time, energy and money.

TYPE STYLE SHEET

Use this sheet as you read through this chapter to keep track of the decisions you make about design and type.

1. The style that best suits the content for my book is:

  ○ conservative ○ serious ○ elegant

  ○ friendly ○ playful ○ lively

  ○ stylish ○ sophisticated ○ trendy

2. The reading audience is:

  ○ children ○ adult readers

3. The size of the finished book will be: (insert measurement)

  _____ (height) x _____ (width)

4. shape: ○ vertical ○ horizontal ○ square

5. Type specifications:

text:

typeface: _____

type size and leading: _____

weight: _____

width: normal

slant: roman

style: not applicable

case: upper and lower case

chapter openings:

typeface: _____

type size and leading: _____

weight: _____

width: _____

slant: _____

style: _____

case: _____

subheads:

typeface: _____

type size and leading: _____

weight: _____

width: _____

slant: _____

style: _____

case: _____

(If there are heads, subheads and then more subheads, keep track of their number and type specs on this sheet.)

photo captions:

typeface: _____

type size and leading: _____

weight: _____

width: _____

slant: _____

style: not applicable

case: upper and lower case

running heads:

typeface: _____

type size: _____

weight: _____

width: _____

slant: _____

style: not applicable

case: upper and lower case

PAGE STYLE SHEET

Use this sheet as you read through this chapter to keep track of the decisions you make about page format.

1. complexity of grid: ○ minimum (go to 2)
                             ○ simple (go to 3)
                             ○ professional (go to 4)

2. minimum grid: text pages:

margins: (insert measurement)   left: _____ right: _____
                                top: _____ bottom: _____

type alignment: ○ left margin   ○ justified   ○ centred

3. simple grid: text pages:

margins: (insert measurement)   left: _____ right: _____
                                top: _____ bottom: _____

type alignment: ○ left margin   ○ justified   ○ centred

page number: ○ top of page   ○ bottom of page
               ○ left margin   ○ centred   ○ right margin

running head: ○ no ○ yes: ○ centred   ○ left margin

4. professional grid: left-hand text pages

margins: (insert measurement)   left: _____ right: _____
                                top: _____ bottom: _____

type alignment: ○ left margin   ○ justified   ○ centred

page number: ○ top of page   ○ bottom of page
               ○ left margin   ○ centred

running head: ○ no ○ yes: ○ centred   ○ left margin

professional grid: right-hand text pages

margins: (insert measurement)   left: _____ right: _____
                                top: _____ bottom: _____

type alignment: ○ left margin   ○ justified   ○ centred

page number: ○ top of page   ○ bottom of page
               ○ centred   ○ right margin

running head: ○ no ○ yes: ○ centred   ○ left margin

5. Does the book have chapters? If yes, chapter opening pages:
margin: (insert measurement from top edge of finished book page
to line on which chapter title/number will be placed) top: _____

type alignment: ○ left margin ○ centred   ○ right margin

page number: ○ bottom of page
       ○ left margin ○ centred   ○ right margin

running head: ○ no

6. Does the book have pictures? If yes, pictures will appear:
       ○ with text (go to 7)
       ○ on their own pages (go to 8)
       ○ in photo sections (go to 9)

7. Pictures in text need:

margins around pictures: left: _____ right: _____
(insert measurement)   top: _____ bottom: _____
captions: ○ yes   ○ no

8. Picture pages need:

margins around pictures: left: _____ right: _____
(insert measurement)   top: _____ bottom: _____
captions: ○ yes   ○ no
page number: ○ no
running head: ○ no

9. Photo section pages need:

margins around pictures: left: _____ right: _____
(insert measurement)   top: _____ bottom: _____
captions: ○ yes
page number: ○ top of page ○ bottom of page
       ○ left margin ○ centred   ○ right margin
running head: ○ yes   ○ no

GOOD TYPE CHOICES FOR YOUR BOOK

Here are some very standard typefaces that are pleasing to the eye. Two alternatives are given for each type of book. Either choice will produce a professional looking use of type: mix and match between recommendations at your peril!

BOOK CATEGORY	Large headings, such as chapter openings:		Small headings, such as recipe names:		Text	
	TYPEFACE	TYPE SIZE	TYPEFACE	TYPE SIZE	TYPEFACE	TYPE SIZE
Family History A	Phaistos	48	Phaistos Bold	16	Berling	11/16
Family History B	Times	48	Times Bold	16	Times	12/16
Cookbook A	Centaur	48	Centaur	32	Centaur	11/15
Cookbook B	Times	36	Times	21	Times	11.5/15
Poetry A	Cochin	36	Cochin Ital	21	Cochin	11/14
Poetry B	Times	36	Times Ital	18	Times	11/14
Children's Juvenile Picture Book A	Improv	48	New Century Schoolbook	24	Helvetica Textbook	16/22
Children's Juvenile Picture Book B	New Century Schoolbook	36	Helvetica Bold	24	Helvetica	16/22
Adult Novel A	Garamond	24	Meta	12	Garamond	11/14
Adult Novel B	Times	21	Times	14	Times	10/13
Self-Help A	Trajan	30	Bembo Bold	13	Bembo	12/16
Self-Help B	Helvetica	26	Helvetica Bold	12	Times	11/16

Source: ArtPlus Design & Communications

CHAPTER 6

WRITING AND DESIGNING A COVER THAT WORKS

Can you tell a book by its cover? One thing is for sure: even though a cover can't give you the complete story about what's on the inside, the cover does tell a lot about the book. Beyond the title, the author's name and possibly his or her credentials, it establishes a style, or tone, for the book. Romantic fiction, for instance, is almost instantly recognizable by the front cover illustration.

Since personal preferences vary wildly, it can be somewhat difficult to pin down exactly what makes a great cover, but it's very easy to identify what makes a bad one. Think about the dreadful covers you've seen: the ones that are hard to read, the ones that use a depressing colour or ugly image, the ones that look like a high-school yearbook. All of these tend to be very effective in creating one response in the beholder: the avoidance response!

You can learn a lot from this. You can learn that you want your book to attract attention and to be welcomed by its readers. The sheer number of great cover designs out there proves that this can be easily accomplished.

COVER vs JACKET

You will determine in Ch. 10 whether you are making a cover or a jacket. But let's quickly summerize: a **cover** is the heavy printed paper encasing the pages of a softcover book, while a **jacket** wraps around the case of a hardcover book. You will probably choose to produce a softcover book. Either way, you'll want the outside of the book to be beautiful.

THE BASICS

Your book **cover** should include:

	At the Minimum	The Maximum
Front	• title	• title
		• subtitle
	• author's name	• author's name
Spine	• title	• title
	• author's surname	• author's surname or whole name
		• logo of publisher
		• publisher's name
Back		• title
		• subtitle
		• back cover copy
		• price
		• ISBN
		• bar code
		• author's credentials

If you're producing a jacket, you have the luxury of the flaps to give the reader all the important selling information. The front jacket flap is used for a repeat of the book title, the price and copy that briefly describes the book. The back flap is used for the author's credentials, often an author photograph, a credit line for the photographer of the author and the publisher's name. Quite often the jacket back only includes an illustration with the ISBN and bar code.

THE FRONT COVER

Since the importance of the front cover is pretty much established, you have good motivation to make yours the best it can be. There are five no-fail rules for good cover design:

1. Keep the design simple.
2. Don't attempt too much colour.
3. Ensure that whatever photograph or illustration you choose to use is of excellent quality.
4. Choose a cover treatment that's appropriate for the subject or nature of the book.
5. If it doesn't work, throw it out and start over.

ADOPT AND ADAPT

It's no crime to find a cover you love on an existing book and adapt its design for your own book. It won't violate the copyright on the published work as long as you do not exactly reproduce the other cover — including its title! You will probably find it much easier to design a cover by mimicking the typeface and style combined with the sort of illustration that appears on the cover you admire and apply your personal adjustments. In the end, these individualized flourishes will make it your own.

RULE ONE: Simplicity

The structure of a front cover is straightforward: the title usually appears in the top third of the cover, and the author's name in the bottom third. This way the title takes a position of prominence because book publishers assume that the subject matter of the book as conveyed by its title is what motivates buyers and, in a book rack, the title will still show! This is usually the case, unless the author is such an expert or so established in the genre (think Tom Clancy) that the author's name alone can sell the book.

So let us assume that you have chosen a great title based on the advice on page 41. Now you must consider fit and legibility. The title has to fit in the space you have available. A title that is too long can create legibility problems. A title that is too short can be meaningless to everyone except its author.

Legibility problems can be created by:

- type that's too small
- type that's too large
- inappropriate typefaces
- type that is printed over an illustration or photograph

The solutions to the first three of these problems are obvious: pick a type size that is large enough to be read easily without being overpowering, don't allow words to hyphenate and don't use fancy typefaces — usually a good standard font like Times is all you need. Avoid script typefaces. Script type is best saved for wedding invitations; no one will be fooled into thinking the cover is handwritten if you use a script face.

Setting type over an illustration, photograph or art of any kind is usually best left to a design expert. It is perfectly acceptable to produce a book cover that does not include any

---

SIMPLICITY IS THE SECRET

A busy cover design is a telltale sign of a self-published book. Remember, the cover doesn't have to tell the whole story — that's what you've got the text pages for. Make your cover easy to read and good to look at.

---

illustrative element. However, if you do build in an illustration or photograph, plan to position your type above the illustration, beside it, or below it. Type that runs over top of an illustration can quickly become illegible.

RULE TWO: Don't Attempt Too Much

Writing a book is quite an accomplishment; expecting to design it so well that you can quit your day job and join the ranks of book designers may be somewhat unrealistic. See Rule One: keep your use of title, type, and layout simple.

Be careful with colour. Remember that without sufficient contrast between the background and the type, the type can't be read. And just as colours connote meanings in other areas of life, so do they in books: dark blues and purples convey richness and authority; black is dramatic and sombre; white is clean and eye-catching; greens are fresh; reds, oranges and yellows are hot! Don't even think about brown. Publishers believe that brown books don't sell, and as a consequence you will not see many brown books on the shelves.

BLACK COVERS

Warning about black: It might look wonderful as a background cover colour but it is more subject to scuffing — rub marks — than any other shade. Once scuffed, the book looks badly used.

RULE THREE: Illustration

You have decided to include a photograph in the centre of the front cover. Let us hope in this case that you own the photo or that it is a stock photo and you've received permission to use it. If not, you must seek permission for the use of any piece of art that you don't own. Consider whether the image is clear, unblemished and true in colour, especially if it is a photograph of a person. A bad photograph or illustration can easily detract from the title or even the contents of the book. Your cover will capture attention all right, but not the kind you want.

Review the guidelines for choice of art and photos for the text on p.67; the same rules will apply for the cover.

If you plan to use an archival family photo in your family history, reserve it for the inside of the book. Unless it is a person of such prominence as to be immediately recognizable by all the members of your family, it will receive better treatment inside the book where a caption can explain all the reader needs to know about the scene, people or person depicted.

As discussed earlier, do not use a "negative" photo, that is, an unpleasant photo of a nasty thing, person or place. Virtually nothing can detract more from a book.

RULE FOUR: Match Your Cover to the Subject

Just as crayon cover art doesn't suit your family history, neither does a dour portrait. It seems obvious that certain books should look certain ways, yet many people apparently miss the point.

It is not clichéd — but rather, appropriate — to make your family history look dignified, your self-help book appear easy to use and understand, and your novel look inviting. Similarly, by all means use pictures of food for your cookbook and crayon art for your children's book.

Yet some folks seem to think that rules are made to be broken. Certainly, if you've got an artistic flair (and this talent is confirmed by others) go ahead and design as you please. Be bold, be brave, and be prepared that — just maybe — your readers won't share your enthusiasm.

RULE FIVE: See Rule One

It happens to the most experienced book designers: They just can't get it right. It happens to publishers too: Their book designers just can't get it right. You'll know when this happens to you, because you won't be happy with the look of the book.

There's only one course of action. Put aside the concept, the colours, the treatment, and start over. Just as you have been wise enough to throw away a sentence in your text that didn't work, you must feel that way about the cover design. A bad

---

AN EASY SOLUTION

You can create a lovely cover by:

1. Making a box shape on paper, either on your computer or by hand. Its shape should conform to the shape of the book, in other words a rectangular book would have a rectangular box.
2. Place your title inside the box, with type styled as you wish.
3. Put a nice border on the box.
4. Develop an overall treatment, either a solid colour or a pattern, for the area outside the text box.
5. Put the box and the background together.

You can start by creating the box shape or start with the overall background: the background could be as simple as a piece of beautiful handmade paper – which you then "tip" (see p.55) your type box onto – or something more complex.

---

cover usually can't be revived, and by throwing it out you'll save yourself the anguish of trying *ad nauseam* slight adjustments that for some reason still don't salvage the work.

Instead, clear your brain, try some more research in your local bookstore, and then let the same inspiration that drove you to put all those words on paper guide you toward making a cover you love.

SPECIFIC RECOMMENDATIONS BY GENRE

Here are some general guidelines for types of cover design.

Children's. An illustration will make the book more attractive. Try using primary colours on a white background. Make the words easy to read; there's usually no need for a subtitle.

Family History. This is a good candidate for a straightforward title, such as "The Yates Family," supplemented with a subtitle such as, "Our History in Canada since 1801". Try using dignified colours such as a creamy white background with type in a dark blue.

Cookbook. You may not need a subtitle, depending on what you call the book. Try to use colours that feel clean and bright, such as lettuce green or tomato red. White makes a particularly good choice for a background.

Self-help. You may want to establish yourself as an authority on your subject, so include a photo of yourself on the front. For business-like topics, use strong business-like colours, not pastels. Often self-help books use very self-explanatory titles — "How to Make a Billion Dollars with My Sure-Thing Stock-Market Tips" — that happen to be quite long. If this is the case, a subtitle would be overkill.

Novel. This book needs an illustration or evocative photograph on the front. Keep it simple. There's no need for a subtitle.

Poetry. Since you're in the word-crafting business anyway, it shouldn't be a problem to find an appropriate title that can be supported with an illustration. It's not necessary, but nice.

Autobiography. You may choose a phrase or words that seem to describe the theme of your life, or part of it, as your title. This is probably the only kind of book that identifies the genre, "An Autobiography," on the front cover. The field is wide open as to how to illustrate or decorate the cover, though using a picture of yourself is going a bit over the top.

THE SPINE

Spines must be functional first and decorative second. Be sure you've got the necessary information in the customary order: title, author, publisher. Make certain that you design the type to fit the space available. Remember, some books, such as those that are saddlestitched (stapled through the spine), handsewn or Cerlox-bound with plastic rings, have no spine.

Then, if you have the space and the creative knack, you can include a photo or illustration. A photo on the spine can be really eye-catching. If you're publishing in a particularly competitive genre, something like this can make your book stand out on the shelf.

THE BACK COVER

While it's very important to engage the reader by the look of the front cover, the back cover must take that interest to the next level. The back cover is a selling proposition, short and sweet. You've got about 100 words to convince readers that this is a book they want to read. The back cover can transform a browser into a buyer.

There are two separate, though related, issues to deal with in putting together the back cover — its overall design and its copy.

BACK COVER DESIGN

Many of the rules about front-cover design also apply to the back of the book: Keep the treatment simple, appropriate to the contents, and easy to read. It's a good idea to keep your type on the large side (say, 14/16 pts). Make sure that the background is light in colour, and the type is dark, so there will be enough contrast between the two to make the words easy to read. If the copy you've written doesn't fit in the space available, edit or rewrite your copy. But don't reduce the type size to squeeze it all in.

Make sure there's lots of space around the words on the back cover — avoid crowding too much on. And finally, if you've styled your type and it doesn't look right, that usually means it's not right. Go to your bookshelf for inspiration and try again!

BACK COVER COPY

The words on the back cover can convince a person to buy a book, or not. It's important that you persevere in writing the copy over and over until it is absolutely perfect.

Different genres structure their copy somewhat differently. This is because some books (for example, self-help or cookbooks) need a lot more copy than others. The copy is organized to avoid long paragraphs of information, which can be very boring to read. To keep the copy snappy, it can be structured into three parts: lead paragraph, bulleted points and closing paragraph.

The lead-off paragraph briefly describes the book: "A practical collection of valuable recipes compiled by one of Canada's best known cooks...." Then the list of bulleted points tells the reader the features of the book:

- 40 kitchen-tested recipes
- the world's best recipe for Triple Chocolate Brownies
- recipes for healthy eating that taste great

The final paragraph often repeats the same message already delivered, but uses slightly different words to emphasize to the reader the benefits of buying the book: "Gathered together for the first time, these tried-and-true recipes will keep your family healthy and happy on special occasions and everyday too!"

Overall the tone should be very upbeat and positive. After all, you're telling people why they should part with their cash and pick your book instead of the competition.

Other books usually have a lot less to say about themselves. A history, autobiography or book of poetry will have back cover copy that is fairly short and provides a descriptive summary of the contents: "*Up the Line* is the story of life in the Ottawa Valley from its earliest settlement in 1802 to today." There is not the same feverish sales pitch because these books are more individual in their contents than are self-help books. Publishers assume the reader will be interested in the book for its information, not just for what it will do for them.

ENDORSEMENTS

Endorsements can be used on the back, or even front, cover of books, especially fiction. These are often obtained by the publisher, who usually has some connection with the person who has been solicited. Providing endorsements can be payback time for an author who "owes one" to a publisher or the author of the work. If you know someone you can ask for an endorsement — someone whose name or credentials (Managing Editor, *Times Literary Supplement*) could influence a reader — then it's a good idea to use such an endorsement. You will need to provide that person with a copy of your complete manuscript and you may need to suggest just what it is you'd like said. It sometimes happens that you will actually write the endorsement yourself and then ask your endorser to put their name to it. Be sure you make it plain to the person providing the endorsement what it will be used for. If your endorser doesn't carry weight in the eyes of the public, it's better to leave off the endorsement.

In the cases of a children's story or adult novel, you should provide a brief description of the story. Adult readers expect a genre to become readily apparent: Is the book romantic fiction, a mystery or science fiction? Get this point across right away, but still keep your copy to one, or at the most two, shortish paragraphs while you establish the salient points of the story. Of course, never give away the ending.

THE PRICE

Establishing the right selling price for your book can be tricky. Too high, and it won't fly off the shelf. On the other hand, a rock-bottom price is not a sure-fire technique for great sales either. Everyone understands why an overpriced book won't sell, but why not an underpriced one? The truth is that people are suspicious of low prices and often regard the product as being inferior.

The very best way to determine your selling price is to review what similar books are selling for and price yours in that range. This assumes that even the top end of that range covers your costs of production and provides you with a profit margin of 10% of the selling price, an amount equivalent to the royalty you would earn in traditional book publishing. If your costs and profit aren't covered, you will either have to sacrifice profits or increase your selling price until you have arrived at a comfort level.

Some books, such as a family history, have no reference selling point. Since you're probably not selling this book anyway, don't include a price on the cover.

THE ISBN AND BAR CODE

The ISBN for the book is repeated on the back cover to simplify the reordering process by bookstores.

The Bar Code is printed on the back for the booksellers to track the book through their ordering/inventory system. It is unlikely as a self-publisher that you will acquire a bar code; the ISBN and your press name is sufficient. You can find book-industry bar code software on the Internet.

AUTHOR'S CREDENTIALS

The credentials of the author sometimes appear on the back cover or, more usually, on the back jacket flap. If you include your credentials, be brief and to the point. If your credentials don't necessarily relate to the work at hand (in other words, you wrote

the book just because you felt like telling a good story) you don't
need to talk about yourself. Let your book speak for you.

A BOOK OF ONE'S OWN COVER

This book began with a cover design much more complex than what you
see now. Our designer, Dave Murphy at ArtPlus, thought that it would be
appropriate to include an illustration or photo of a book. Unfortunately,
we just couldn't find an illustration that felt right. After several tries, the
all-type treatment suggested by our senior editor at the publishing house
seemed the best route.

TEMPLATES

The templates in the appendix will give you some ideas for
structuring your front cover.

CHAPTER 7

GETTING READY TO PRINT

Now that you have the manuscript written, the book designed and pages made up to your satisfaction, either on your own printer, typewriter or designer's system, the fun part begins. The part called book production, in which the pages become a printed book. The part that thousands of writers hope to achieve and so very few actually do.

And yet, book production is not an intimidating task; you'll find many people willing to give you a hand — from the person at the copy shop who'll be photocopying your colour covers (if you go that route) to your printer's sales rep(if you go with one). But if you know the basics that follow in these chapters, you'll be in a much better position to assess the value of that help and make the appropriate decisions.

THE IMPORTANCE OF PLANNING

There are two factors to take into consideration as you begin to plan the production of your book: how many copies of the finished book you need to suit your purpose, which is called the print run, and how many pages will be in your book. These factors will determine which method of reproduction and binding is right for you.

The Print Run

How many books do you want? You will need to know this to accurately plan print production. Make a list of who you will give the book to, because even if you intend to sell the book, there will still be a number of family members and friends, for instance, to whom you will undoubtedly want to give a copy.

Maybe you plan to only give your book away. Even so, that list will help you make sure you haven't forgotten someone, and it will help to focus your thoughts about where the copies are going once the book is actually completed.

If your plans include selling the book, be modest in your assessment of how many copies you need to start with. There are two good reasons for this: firstly, you can always print more books if you run out, and secondly, you won't tie up a chunk of cash unnecessarily in the expense of printing (and in storage later). Please refer to Chapter 12 for a discussion of going to market.

The Number of Pages

Book printers print in "forms". At one time, forms were a frame in which metal type was fastened to allow printing or plate making. Now, such frames aren't used, but the word "forms" persists. Books are comprised of sections, called forms, that consist of eight pages, or a multiple of eight. Thus you should plan your book to meet this requirement.

While it is true that, if you're printing the pages yourself on a computer printer or having them photocopied, you are not restricted to forms, if you do change your method of production to offset printing, it is much easier to have the book organized this way from the beginning than to go back and try and force it into forms. Who is not to say that your first printing won't be such a success that you won't be going back to increase your print run? Planning in forms can just make book production easier in the long run.

THE NEAREST EIGHT

You can make your book either come up or go down to the nearest eight by using a few tricks in the publishing trade:

- Add a half-title page. This is the very first page in the book. Instead of being a proper title page, it shows only the title of the book. It's followed by a blank on its reverse, adding two pages to your total.
- Add a dedication page. There's usually someone in a writer's life who merits such a reward. Again, it is usually followed by a blank, making it good for two pages.
- Add a foreword or introduction (a definition of each can be found in *The Chicago Manual of Style*). These usually add at least two pages.
- Start each new chapter on a right-hand page. This can add many pages, depending on your chapter count.
- Start the index on a right-hand page and enlarge the type size used for the index. This can bring the pages up by three or more.
- As a last resort, add blanks at the end. Unbelievable as it may seem, it is often more economical to include these unprinted pages than it is to end the book in what (to a printer) is an odd number of pages.

Alternatively, if you have included any of the first three elements in your book, you can remove them to bring down the page count to that magic number of the eight multiple.

Many books are "folio'd," that is, their pages are numbered so as to make it appear that this rule of eight is not in effect. However, if you combine the numbered text pages with the sometimes unnumbered (or sometimes numbered in roman numerals) preliminary pages, you will virtually always arrive at a multiple of eight.

Though the number of pages is driven by the content, remember two things while developing your book, because they affect the number of pages:

1. Paper is expensive. If there's ever doubt as to the contribution of an element of the book and, just maybe, that element doesn't really add to the overall strength of the work, leave it out. It will not only save you the additional expense of the extra paper and ink for printing, it will probably make the book stronger editorially too.

2. Despite number 1, never compromise the important elements of design to fit more words onto each page. Yes, you can reduce the number of pages this way, but cramming too much type on the page is a mistake you don't want to make.

HOW TO PUT QUANTITY AND SIZE TOGETHER

The following chart brings together both size of the print run with the number of pages to help you decide whether your book is suitable for reproduction by hand, digitally, or by offset printing.

This chart is only a guideline. While it is quite possible to saddlestitch (meaning stapled two or three times through the centre fold of the book), 750 copies of the eight-page recipe

No. of Copies	No. of Pages						
	8	16	32	64	96	128–356	356+
1–9							
10–24							
25–99							
100–499							
500 +							

Handmade | Digital Reproduction | Offset Printing

book you prepared, the overriding assumption is that you are simply going to choose a more efficient method of putting these pages together. This chart is based on that notion.

Handmade

Handmade doesn't necessarily mean tacky. There are many beautiful works of book art that have been made by their authors in just such small quantities. In the following chapter we'll describe how you can easily reproduce the pages of your book, add a cover and bind both together for posterity.

Digital

Digital reproduction includes everything from good old photocopying to high-tech digital printing.

In this "between" zone you've got plenty of room for creativity, because digital printing offers lots of flexibility. In Chapter 9 we will describe the methods of digital reproduction.

Offset

Ah, every author's dream: to be going to press. Offset printing, with its corresponding binding options, is the traditional book-manufacturing route. You'll find how to navigate this procedure in Chapter 10.

There are other options, particularly for binding, that aren't covered here. You could decide, for instance, to three-hole punch your book pages and insert them in binders. Binders are a good utilitarian way of holding a lot of pages together, but using a binder produces, well... a binder, not what is customarily considered to be "a book". So, our attention in the following pages will be focused on producing a book — in its more-or-less usual interpretation — of your own.

COST VS. LOST OPPORTUNITY

The cost of producing a book is not only in continual flux because of ups and downs in the paper market, but also — as you're about to appreciate in the following pages — because there are so many variables.

It is only to be expected that whatever you do yourself is the cheapest; after all, you're the labour! Therefore, by extrapolation, the handmade method is the least expensive. The cost for digital printing is higher and the cost for a manufactured book the highest.

Yet perhaps it's not fair to book printers to single them out as the most expensive route for production. Offset may cost the most, but the finished product has production values that other forms usually can't match. When you're thinking about which method of production is the best given your ultimate plans for your book, it may be worthwhile to factor in professional appearance versus the dollars involved. In all likelihood, you will want your book to look good and be durable, whether the market is friends, family or the local bookshop. It doesn't matter if you're giving the book away or selling it, if it doesn't measure up, then you haven't saved money at all.

CHAPTER 8

MADE BY
HAND

In the previous chapter we determined that making your book by hand was the best option if your book has 64 pages or less, and if you wanted less than 100 copies for distribution.

Handmade books are an art form that has been on the wane since Mr. Gutenberg printed his first volume in the 15th century. You should take real pride in the task before you, because the results can be beautiful, even if you feel you are artistically challenged!

The process of making a book by hand begins with deciding how to put the words on the page. Then you must determine how to reproduce the pages in the book, how to produce an attractive cover and finally how to bind the pages and cover together.

REPRODUCTION MUST START WITH AN ORIGINAL

Before you can have multiple copies of a book, you must start with one good version which we will call the original. It is from the original that the copies are made. When you are producing a hand-made book, there are three ways to go about creating the original:

- handwriting
- a typewriter
- a computer linked to a laser printer

Handwriting

Before printing was invented, every single book was written by hand. Scribes prided themselves on the beauty of their handwriting, and by combining words with decorative elements, called illumination, they created magnificent books that were enjoyed by a select few.

Although extremely rare, handwriting the pages in your book is still an option, if the handwriting is up to the task.

Handwritten pages are especially suitable for poetry, and, sometimes, as printing in a children's book. The key to a successful handwritten book is not to have too many words on each page. Quite often one sees recipe books compiled as fundraisers in which all the ingredients and cooking instructions have been handwritten. The writing compels your attention, so that you don't see how good the recipes might be. This points to the biggest problem with handwriting the text: the handwriting can detract — or distract — from the content.

CALLIGRAPHY

The art of beautiful handwriting has made a real resurgence over the past few years. Many craft shops, stationers and even toy shops stock the tools of the trade for those who want to try their hand at this art form.

Calligraphy could be wonderful on book pages, whether created by you or by someone you hire. It would be especially appropriate to use when decorative type is called for: the title of the book, the chapter names or even the names of recipes.

If you are going to handwrite your text you will want to:

1. Make sure your handwriting, or the printing of your child in the case of a children's book, is absolutely legible.

2. Try to keep the writing consistent throughout all the pages: use the same pen, write on the same surface and try to form your letters in a similar style throughout.

3. Don't print everything in capital letters: in the e-mail world this is called shouting — and for good reason — because it is just too heavy-handed.

4. Be neat. Rule your pages very lightly, using a non-reproducing blue pencil or hard lead pencil to keep your writing on an even keel. If you make a mistake, it's better to do the page over than erase. This is for posterity, remember!

5. Keep all your margins the same on every page. Medieval monks used to plan their pages before committing ink to parchment by carefully calculating how the words would fit on the page. You should do the same. Then you won't be left with one last page and only two words to fill it!

Plan to handwrite one perfect copy and then reproduce it following the advice below. Don't try to write multiple copies: there are, simply, better ways of producing copies than individually handwriting them.

Typewriting

Despite what some advocates of computer technology would have us think, there are still many people who only have access to a typewriter. A typewriter can be a quite acceptable way of producing pages, especially if it is electric.

Typewritten pages are acceptable choices for a poetry, family history, or any short work.

If you are going to typewrite your text:

1. Put in a new ribbon and keep putting in new ribbons if the book is a longish one to keep the type consistently black throughout the book.
2. Buy a new jar of liquid corrector, or a new erasing ribbon to fix mistakes neatly.
3. Don't type all in capital letters.
4. Use a good dictionary to hyphenate words correctly.
5. Leave lots of space between the rows of type. A page filled from top to bottom margin with row upon row of typewritten words does not invite reading. Make good use of white space. (See Chapter 5.)

Duplicating Handwritten or Typewritten Originals

Once you have your handwritten or typewritten original completed, take it to your local copy shop for duplication. You will have to choose between one- or two-sided copying. One-sided will always look like a collection of loose pages; two-sided more closely approximates printing. If you choose the latter, make certain that the two pages "back up" properly — that is, that their margins match and the type from one page overlays the type on the other when viewed together. Imagine holding the page up to the light: you will want the type to cover the same area on each side of the page.

The real bonus to photocopying as a method of duplication is that, unlike the case with offset printing, you are not bound by forms. Therefore your book does not have to be in the multiple of eight, because it is not being produced on a press.

Computer/Laser Printer

Well, there's just no way around this: The computer/laser print-er combination is the best way to produce an original for every kind of book. Not only do you have an enormous array of typefaces and type sizes available, but mistakes can be fixed without a trace.

Plus, this is the one case when you can actually produce more than a single copy of the pages, and still keep sane. If you're producing, say, a half-dozen copies of an eight-page recipe book that gathers Mom's favourites, just print off all the copies of the pages you need and save the expense of going elsewhere.

If you are printing the pages of a book that will be saddle-stitched (again, this means stapled two or three times through the centre fold of the book) — whether you are printing the pages off your computer or you are taking them to a photocopy shop that will reproduce the pages — you will need to set your pages up in "printer's spreads". This is because you are not pro-ducing single pages of the book but double pages. Double pages are called spreads.

You can very easily calculate these spreads for yourself. Simply fold together pieces of paper that will result in the cor-rect number of pages in your book and write the page number on each page. Remember that each sheet of paper yields four book pages. When you take them apart you will find that the paper looks like this (for a 16-page book):

1st sheet: side 1		reverse		2nd sheet: side 1		reverse	
page no.	page no.	page no.	page no.	page no.	page no.	page no.	page no.
16	1	2	15	14	3	4	13

3rd sheet: side 1		reverse		4th sheet: side 1		reverse	
page no. 12	page no. 5	page no. 6	page no. 11	page no. 10	page no. 7	page no. 8	page no. 9

Then stack the sheets with page 1 on top, followed by 3, 5, 7 and 9 and your book will be perfectly paged.

To achieve printer's spreads on your laser printer you will be printing on your page horizontally (usually called landscape orientation) to create two book pages side by side on each piece of paper. By using paper that is 8-1/2 x 14" you will be able to produce a book with a finished size of about 6-1/2 x 8-1/2" (not 7- x 8-1/2") because you need some extra space to trim the pages. More on this later. You may need to buy a paper tray for your printer that can handle the longer length, but it's worth the expense to save the aggravation — and paper waste — of feeding individual sheets through on a shorter tray.

If you are not saddlestitching the book, you will be producing single pages that will be sewn, wiro- or Cerlox-bound. To do this, simply print out a single page for every page in the book, or multiple copies if the number of books you're producing is few. Cerlox or wiro- binding is usually done at a photocopy shop. If you're handsewing, see page 113.

When printing from a laser printer, make sure to use proper laser paper, not photocopy paper or bond paper. Laser paper really makes a big difference to the print quality.

A final word: If you do not have access to a laser printer, set up your "print file" on a floppy disk and take it to a service bureau such as a photocopy shop, where it can be output to a laser printer. When you've come this far, don't sell yourself short by using a lower-quality printer.

COVER UPS

Now that you've got the inside pages finished, you will need to select a cover material (this heavy paper is known as cover stock) that is attractive, and appropriate for the finished product. You also need to choose one that is suitable for the binding method you have in mind.

Creating the Handmade Book Cover

There are three ways you can easily create a cover for your book.

1. The Do-It-Yourself Method: Draw your own cover art or design the cover on your computer and print it out. If you're producing more than one copy, you'll have to duplicate the original. Photocopying, whether in colour or black and white, is probably your best bet. Affix the cover art to your cover stock.

2. Use preprinted materials to give an overall pattern for the cover. Affix this material to stock that is suitable for use as a cover.

3. Die-cut either plain or preprinted paper (see page 110 about die-cutting) to reveal an illustration or the title on the first page of the book.

Do-It-Yourself

Following all the advice in this book you have created front-cover art that makes you happy. Whether you have done this by hand or machine makes no difference as long as it works for you.

> ## THE LOOK OF CANVAS, ON PAPER
>
> If you are printing your covers off your computer, and your design includes a colour photograph or illustration, you might want to look into a product by Xerox called Canvas Paper. This paper has a texture like the canvas used in oil painting. Used properly, the effects of printing on such paper can be quite beautiful.

Duplicate the number of copies of the art that you need for the number of copies you are producing, and make yourself a couple of spares in case you need to experiment or there's an accident during the binding process. You can make these copies by printing in colour from your computer, taking your file on disk to a service bureau where they can print it in colour for you, or by colour photocopying.

The paper you use for the cover for your book can be either the same weight as the text paper, or, for greater durability and a more professional appearance, a heavier weight paper. Heavier stock also gives the option of die-cutting, which is not really possible with text-weight paper.

A very accessible choice for a heavier stock is any card–type stock, such as Bristol board. Cut the board to the size you need. Remember, in a saddlestitched book this board is going to wrap around the entire book. You will want to apply your front cover art to the part of the board that will become the front cover, using either spray adhesive or rubber cement. If you have prepared back cover art, it needs to go on too. Be careful that you apply the "art" so that it is square and properly aligned. Then, by using a wonderful product called GEO Multi Fix Adhesive Film you can add a smooth shiny finish to the cover, giving it the look of lamination. Multi Fix is available in well-equipped office supply stores and is very inexpensive. Although Multi Fix claims to be removable, it does tend to also remove part of the top layer of the paper to which it has been adhered when you lift it. Therefore, it's a good idea to experiment with some first, so when you lay it down you can just leave it there.

VIEW OF THE OUTSIDE COVER OF A
SADDLESTITCHED BOOK SHOWING COPY LAYOUT

Back Cover   Front Cover

If you're making a saddlestitched book, you'll then have to prepare the "cover" for folding at its centre line. Bristol board can be ugly when folded unless you score it first. To score the board, first draw a line where you want the board to fold. Then, using a straight edge and a blunt, but pointed, instrument such as a letter opener or unopened pair of scissors, run the instrument lightly along the straight edge, making a faint crease in the board. This is called scoring. Be careful not to actually cut the board. You might have to score the line several times until the board will fold easily and neatly. However, don't fold it closed yet. Wait until you've place your pages inside, and have inserted the staples through the spine. Then, fold the book closed.

If you are handsewing or Cerlox-binding the book, you will be dealing with two sheets of "cover" paper instead of the wrap-around sheet you use in saddlestitching. Bristol board with your art and Multi Fix on top is still a good route to go for the front cover. Although you could dispense with the back cover, it's a nice finishing touch to put a heavy-weight stock on the back that gives the work a more solid feel.

Preprinted Materials

Preprinted materials include an enormous variety of possibilities: wallpaper, handmade paper, fabric, Con-Tact®, gift wrap — you name it. Such paper generally becomes the design of the cover, as it would look odd to add type on over such overall patterns. However, type can go in a type box and then be pasted over the pattern of your material.

However, frequently such materials are so beautiful that they make a powerful statement on their own. This is your personal decision.

To use such materials, you will probably have to laminate them to a sturdier stock. Experiment with rubber cement, starch paste and spray adhesive to see which works successfully. Once applied to the standard cover stock, the preprinted material cover is treated like any other.

Die-cutting

In true die-cutting, a metal die stamps its way through the material being die cut. This creates a hole in the shape of the die. You're obviously not going to create a metal die, but with an X-acto blade, steady hand and your imagination you can create wonderful die-cut designs and patterns.

In die-cutting you are using both the cover and the first book page to create your design art. The art will be a combination of the shape of the hole being cut in the cover and the colour or illustration on the first book page which appears through the hole.

Die-cutting, in effect, is using a negative image (a hole) in a very positive way. The hole can become the design (if the die-cutting is done in the shape of the sun and stars, for instance), or the hole can reveal the design (if the hole shows an illustration on the page). You can combine die-cutting with the use of preprinted materials for a number of interesting effects.

To die-cut successfully, you really need a paper with some body, so plan to use Bristol board with Multi Fix on top. Plan your design carefully. If the die-cut comes too close to the spine or outside edges of the book, it can weaken the strength of the cover.

Die-cutting offers tremendously exciting possibilities, but it is a true one-off procedure. Every cover you do this way will be an original, so you might want to use this technique only when a very few number of copies are being produced.

A BINDING SITUATION

Ah, yet more choices to make! You're probably getting a good sense of why publishing is such a creative endeavour.

If we return to the section of our original matrix (p. 99) that indicated we were going to make a book by hand because of the number of copies and number of pages in the book, we can now work within those parameters to arrive at a logical way of binding the pages and cover together.

Saddlestitching is a good durable way of holding the pages and cover together. It is inexpensive, and looks professional. After all, publishers produce saddlestitched books all the time, particularly for the children's market.

No. of Copies	No. of Pages					
	8	16	32	64		Saddlestitching
1–9						
10–24						Handsewing
25–99						Fasteners or Cerlox

In saddlestitching, two or three staples are forced through the centre fold of the book from the cover into the middle of the book. This way, the rough edges of the staples are buried on the inside of the book.

You will have had to plan saddlestitching your book from the start of the production process to ensure that you have prepared your text in printer's spreads (see page 105) and your cover as a wraparound. With that done, it is a simple matter to attach your pages to the cover on the top and bottom edges with paper clamps, slide the stapler in to where it is properly positioned to staple through the centre of the book, and apply two or three staples at regular intervals. (If the span of the stapler is too short to reach the centre of the book, you'll have to find a bigger one. You can buy a stapler that's big enough or have your stapling done at a copy shop.)

When you fold your book in half, the pages in the middle of the book are going to protrude. This is called shingling. Printers have all kinds of fancy ways of dealing with this, but for the home publisher it is best to simply allow yourself a good wide margin on all the pages in the book and, using a really good paper cutter, trim that vertical edge so that all the pages line up evenly.

Your saddlestitched book is now complete!

Handsewing

Handsewing is a way of attaching loose sheets with their covers. The best technique for handsewing is called the Japanese binding stitch. But before you get out your needle, you will have to produce five absolutely aligned holes in each complete book you plan to sew. With some patience this can be achieved. First, make a master sheet, with the holes in place. Using the master, and lining up the pages carefully every time, mark the holes on your pages. Then, if you want a very fine binding, use an awl to create the actual holes in the pages. You can make bigger holes by using a single-hole paper punch.

Whatever size hole you end up with, you will want to match the sewing thread accordingly. Embroidery thread would be lovely with small holes, but plastic lacing, also called "gimp," or even a shoelace would be more suitable for large holes. It would be very appropriate to handsew a cookbook with butcher string! One word of caution: The thread should not have much give to it, or with any degree of use the binding will become very sloppy.

The illustration below gives all you need to know to master the binding stitch. Start at the back and you will end at the back; knot the ends neatly and securely. Just make sure you use a long enough piece of thread, rope or lacing to begin with: All this back and forth sewing eats up the thread very quickly.

Cerlox or Fasteners

Virtually any copy shop can provide Cerlox binding. It's cheap, and it does allow the pages in the book to lie flat. For this reason, it's quite popular for cookbooks and other instructional guides.

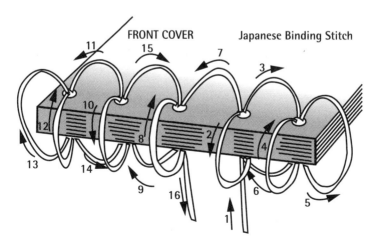

However, it just isn't very good-looking and it can fall apart quite quickly if one or two rings are inadvertently pulled out.

Instead of Cerlox binding, have your book and cover three-hole punched at your local copy shop, or do it yourself. Inserting brass fasteners through the holes makes a very simple, long-lasting but handsome way of holding the book together.

Another alternative is to use grommets. Again, you will need to have your pages pre-punched with holes. Using a grommet tool, insert the grommets into the holes and lock them in place. Grommets are available in a number of colours, any of which are very attractive. You will need to monitor the thickness of your book closely to ensure that the grommets will fit — and hold.

Regardless of what binding option you choose, by taking the time to plan your production carefully — from the design of the pages and cover through their duplication — you will be able to produce a professional-looking handmade book that may well become a family heirloom.

CHAPTER 9

THE TECHNOLOGICAL PRINTING SOLUTION

It may lack the poetry of making a book by hand, and the ease of giving a disk to a printer with a purchase order, but technology in the form of digital printing gives you an efficient and professional way of producing a book.

FINDING A DIGITAL PRINTER

There are photocopy shops around that call themselves digital printers, when in fact they photocopy the pages of your book in just the same way that you would if you had a photocopy machine at your disposal. Then there are digital printers who offer very high-end solutions to digital printing. You will want to make sure you match your needs to what is available.

You can find digital printers in the *Yellow Pages*. You should call a few to discuss your project and get a cost quotation.

If your book is being reproduced in black only, the photocopy shop is the answer. On the other hand, if you have included colour pages of art, photos or illustrations, you should look to the more sophisticated digital printer.

THE PHOTOCOPY SHOP

Photocopy equipment can print on paper that is either 8-1/2 x 11", 8-1/2 x 14" or 11 x 17". The large size allows you to make up your pages in a printer's spread format, as shown on page 105, if two facing pages can be accommodated on one sheet of paper. In this way, you will enjoy the cost savings of "printing" two pages with one click.

Clicks are how photocopy shops price their work: every copy is a click. Using good old white bond paper, about the lowest per click cost is $0.035, so if your book has 100 pages and you need 100 copies, the photocopying cost will be $175 (with two pages per click). If you upgrade the kind of paper you use, that cost will be additional, as will the cost of covers and binding.

BOTH SIDES NOW

If you deliver single pages to the photocopy shop for duplicating, make sure the paper is photocopied double-sided for a more appropriate book-type appearance. It's also a good idea to see how your pages "back up" — that is, the type should cover the same area on the page front and back. If this isn't happening correctly, you may need to have the setup adjusted in the copying or — horrors! — go back to your page setup to make the necessary changes.

Covers can be colour copied on a coated (shiny) or uncoated (not shiny) card stock. Binding options include Cerlox, wiro-binding or coil binding; thermal binding and, occasionally, perfectbinding. Thermal binding uses a tape that is affixed along the spine of the book to hold the pages together. The maximum number of pages that can be bound with thermal binding is about 125.

Among the many advantages of the photocopy route is the speed with which your book can be produced and your ability to make as few copies of the book as you need. You can have just one book copied and bound, and, if the shop isn't busy, that book could be ready in a day. When you need another, back you go. Even though the cost is higher on a per-copy basis to copy one set of pages instead of 100, you won't be out of pocket in the meantime.

The photocopy route might be especially fitting if your book is a "work in progress". Let's say you want to get as much of that family history as you have written to date duplicated and distributed in order to seek contributions from far-away family members. Then it's a great idea to take as much of your book as you have ready and prepare it in a professional, well-designed manner to encourage relatives to read it. Photocopy these pages, Cerlox bind them and send them out. When the comments, new stories and queries come back and your manuscript is finally complete, you may decide that another method of duplication best suits your long-term purpose.

DIGITAL PRINTING

True digital printing is very similar to offset printing because, unlike photocopying, the ink used for printing is a liquid and not a powder. However, unlike offset printing, a laser puts a new image on the plate with every revolution of the press. This makes every page an original.

Digital printing offers many more options than photocopying. Paper size can be up to 12 x 18", and a wide variety of different types of paper are available. Stocks can include those that are coated; they are the ideal choice for the reproduction of colour.

And this is where digital printing shines. This technology prints colour beautifully. Meanwhile, your print run can be only one copy, though a larger run would be far more economical. What's more, you are spared one of the largest expenses in producing a colour book: the film from which the plates are made. Digital printing uses disks instead of film.

There are a number of requirements to meet in the correct preparation of the disk for digital printing. It's best for you to go over this in detail with a sales representative at the digital printer to ensure that your application can be supported (i.e., that the printer is able to work with the program you are using) and that you are preparing your disk to the printer's specifications.

To find a digital printer, you will need to find a supplier with an Indigo press. Though there are not many in Canada, Gandalph Graphics in Toronto (416-750-2324) has an Indigo press that they use in conjunction with a large book printing company. They find many publishers who need just a few copies for review or approval purposes are well satisfied by printing their book on the Indigo and then moving the unbound books into the printing environment to be professionally bound.

This may be the ideal solution for you if you want to produce a small run of a full-colour book.

Also you may want to consider printing the cover of your book this way. You will achieve a much better result than photocopying, and you can still match up your cover to your pages, which have been printed elsewhere, for binding as you choose.

BINDING

How you will bind your digitally reproduced book — whether photocopied or digitally printed — will depend entirely on the number of pages in your book, whether it is formatted for saddle-stitching and how many copies of the book you have produced.

Binding a few copies with few pages in each is addressed in Chapter 8 under the discussion of making books by hand. Binding more copies of many pages is addressed in Chapter 10 about offset printing.

A BOOK FOR EVERYONE

So, what about the Internet as a technological solution? Well, the point about publishing in cyberspace is that it doesn't give you a book of your own. A virtual book lacks the physical presence that real paper, ink (or toner!) and binding delivers. However, the Internet can provide a perfect solution for some home published projects, such as a family history that you want to make available to your family, wherever they may be, at no cost to them.

To "publish" your book this way, you will need to establish a web site through your Internet provider. They will allocate space on their server for your web site and its address. To design your web site, you should buy one of the excellent books precisely on this subject and follow its advice. Search on the Internet itself for web site design information. There are also many software programs that you can use to design your site. Regardless of the tool you use to create your site, the fundamentals of "publishing" your book there will remain constant: You will be able to format your manuscript to look like a book, with headings and subheadings and photos, or art, too, but you will be limited to the use of web-based type fonts. Another problem arises when the person accessing the site downloads the book to print its pages. Their system will override yours. So, if you've gone to some lengths to use interesting fonts and type treatments, it may be for naught.

The Internet as a publishing medium will undoubtedly mature, and many of its current limitations will be overcome. Nevertheless, there are interesting possibilities now — some of which might suit you.

CHAPTER 10

OFFSET PRINTING: GOING TO PRESS

It seems pretty reasonable to assume that, if you want hundreds of copies or more of your book, you're going to do more than give it to your family and friends. This quantity, and the implied assumption of distribution through sales channels, demands the highest degree of professionalism in your approach to printing and binding. After all, your book needs to look credible in order to attain the level of acceptance you're seeking. You need a professional book printer.

HOW TO FIND A PRINTER

As with most things in life, a recommendation from another customer is the best way of finding a company that you'll feel confident working with. But, if you're on your own in this department, and most self-publishing authors are, there are several sources to which you can turn.

The Book Trade in Canada is a reference book that your library should have; it includes a section on Printers, Binders & Related Services. This section lists many of the big players, but even if only a large printer is located in your area, that company could refer you to a small press for your printing.

Scott's Directories is another library reference that can help. All types of business activities are categorized by SIC code number. Book printers are found under the SIC code 2732. Scott's will give the company contact information you'll need for names, phone and fax numbers and address.

Your local *Yellow Pages* can help you find printers, though the ads may not specify which firms are *book* printers. This will be the most difficult list to wade through; however, with any luck, you'll get some advice on finding a book company by speaking with a sales rep at any firm listed.

QUESTIONS TO ASK A PRINTER

Once you're clear that the quantity of books you want requires a book printer, you should start calling printers to obtain cost quotations.

If you've had to pick some printing companies at random from your *Yellow Pages*, you need to establish some groundwork for the type of printing they do. Then you'll be ready to proceed with the specifics of whether your needs and their services match.

Ask:

May I speak to someone in the sales department?

This is the place to start your discussion about your book. Printers' sales reps are very knowledgeable about book production. Usually book printers are enormously helpful, especially when you are just learning about book manufacturing. Tell the person you speak to that you are self-publishing; it will help to focus the conversation on your needs versus those of a publishing company.

Do you manufacture books?

Manufacturing a book means the capability to carry out the entire process of producing a book. In theory, all printers could print the pages of a book, but if they have no way of binding the pages, because they usually print flyers, brochures or other loose-leaf materials, then they are not book manufacturers. It is best to avoid printing pages in one place, and binding the pages in another. Keep looking until you find a book manufacturer: It will make your job easier, and a lot more fun, if there are people to work with who understand books and who will share the benefit of their experience with you.

Can you print the quantity of books I need?

This point should come out almost immediately in your discussion with the sales rep. Some printers specialize in large print runs; others can do very modest amounts. Their willingness to print a small run may also be directly related to the time of year you plan to print. From July through early December, book printers are frantically filling publishers' orders. Their ability or willingness to accommodate you during this period may be limited, because the presses are running full out on large (read: profitable) runs. Come January or February, it may be a different story. Presses are idle and manufacturers are looking for work. At such a time, they may well be prepared to do a small printing.

THE BEST TIME?

Printing in the first quarter of the year may have its advantages in both the cost of the printing and the manufacturers' willingness to take on your job. If you plan to sell your book, remember that fall is the peak season for book sales and delivery to fill these sales usually occurs in August or September. If you plan to give away your book at Christmas, there may be a ten-month lapse between printing and your need for finished books. In other words, you've got a storage problem. Weigh the cost and inconvenience of storage against the savings in printing cost to see if you really are better off to print sooner instead of later.

How long will it take to deliver the finished book?

To answer this, the printer will need details on what type of book you plan to manufacture. These are called the "specifications" and are covered below in detail. However, you should generally calculate between four weeks to three months for finished books. Again, there are many variables affecting this process, such as the format in which you are delivering materials to the printer (for instance, whether you are supplying scanned photos on a disk or originals, which the printer will need to either scan or otherwise shoot); the complexity of the printing (one colour or four?); anything special you want in your book, such as those handmade marbleized endpapers that must be custom ordered from Italy, and the time of year. However, if time is an issue to you because you want the book for a certain date, tell the printer this when you are discussing the job. If time has become short, your choices in finding a printer — and how much you will have to pay — may be affected.

What are your payment terms?

Be prepared to pay for your order when you confirm the job with the printer, whether by a letter or a purchase order. Many printers have lost significant amounts of money when established publishers go out of business, so they will rarely risk investing their time and materials for payment at the end of the process when it is an individual, or even a small company, ordering the work.

What about your risk? Is there a chance that the book won't meet your expectations and you'll have paid for a product you're not satisfied with? The answer when working with an experienced book manufacturer is "no." If you have correctly specified what you want and when you want it, there should be no surprises. If, on the other hand, your printer is dear old Uncle Bob's almost-best friend who runs a small press in his basement, you must guard yourself against the worst. Insist on viewing work samples before starting, and then negotiate payment terms. Terms are often based on paying some money up front, some on completion of printing and some on completion of binding. Your approvals along the way will ensure that you know what you're getting.

A BOOK PRINTER OR A BOOK MANUFACTURER?

The word "printer" is used synonymously with "manufacturer". Manufacturer is actually the correct term, because there is much more to the process of making a book than printing it, but, like so much in the publishing business that hinges on the traditional, "printer" is preferred.

READY TO QUOTE

There are many, many variables in developing an accurate cost quotation for the manufacture of a book. Unless you're one of the lucky few to whom cost is no object, you will want to plan out your specifications carefully, then circulate them to at least three manufacturers for comparison. In publishing houses, it isn't necessarily the cheapest quote which gets the job; it will often be the company that has earned the work through the quality of service it offers. This same factor might affect your decision, too.

Here are the headings you should have on your Request for Quotation:

Title: _____

Quantity: _____

Size of the finished book (trim size): _____

Number of pages: _____

Preparation: Text, cover and/or jacket: _____

Paper: Text: _____

If softcover: Paper: Cover: _____

If hardcover: Materials: Case _____

Paper: Jacket _____

Paper: Endpapers _____

Printing: Text: _____

If softcover: Printing: Cover: _____

If hardcover: Printing: Case: _____

Printing: Jacket: _____

Printing: Endpapers: _____

Binding: _____

Finished Book Date: _____

Shipping: _____

Here's how to complete the information under each heading:

Title

This is simply a way of keeping track of what is being quoted at the manufacturer's. If you haven't decided on a title, just use your name.

Quantity

Now this is essential information to know up front, and while you can change your mind about how many copies of the book you want, it really is discourteous to go back to the printer over and over again with a different quantity each time.

Think quantity through carefully. True, you may not have any idea how much your book will cost, but it will not be cheap, no matter how you produce it. Paper is an expensive commodity. So, who is your market? How realistic are your goals? For some guidance on this subject, refer to the final chapter in this book. Meanwhile, be conservative. If you start small, and your book is a runaway success, you can always have the thrill of going back to press for more copies. This is a great feeling compared to looking at hundreds of "extra" books in permanent storage in your basement.

Also remember that printing is subject to overages and underages. Overages are caused because the press simply can't be stopped at exactly the number of copies you want, and underages are caused for the same reason in addition to some books being destroyed during binding. Printers may specify 10% either way on your quantity to provide this allowance. At the end of the day, you're going to pay for overages, so be prepared for the additional expense.

Size

Trim size is how printers describe the size of the finished book. You have already determined the trim size that is appropriate to the type of book you are producing, but it still makes sense to ask your printer about whether the trim size you've selected is a good fit for their presses. If it isn't, you'll probably see that fact reflected in the cost quotation, and it can explain why one printer's quote will be substantially higher than another's. You just may need to keep shopping for the printer that's right for you.

Number of pages

As discussed in Chapter 7, books are planned to be printed in forms comprised of eight pages. Specify your number of pages rounded up or down to the nearest multiple of eight.

Preparation – Text, Cover and/or Jacket

If you are producing a four-colour text, cover or jacket (see page 133), it's likely that you'll need to have the film for those elements produced at a company that specializes in producing film for printing. This kind of company is called a film house, and one can be located through a recommendation from the printer or your *Yellow Pages*. Coordinate your efforts between the film house and printer to ensure that you are delivering film to the printer's specification.

If your text or cover isn't in four colours, you'll have to deliver the text and cover to the printer in the format they need to produce plates. As discussed in Chapter 5, some printers might ask for camera-ready art (a somewhat antiquated expectation but still a possibility). The better the camera-ready art you supply, the better the printing will be. That is why printers like a good-quality original from which they will make film. This film is then used to make the printing plates. However, camera-ready art can be even a handwritten or typewritten manuscript, with an envelope of photographs the printer must shoot separately and combine with the text. In printer's parlance this is called "stripping," as in "The photos will have to be stripped in." This has traditionally all been part of the printing process.

Now, printers prefer to receive the text files electronically on disk or even by e-mail, with the photos or art already incorporated. You should accompany the electronic file with a paper-copy printout and before you prepare the whole disk, make up a sample of a chapter or two to see if the disk is being prepared correctly and that all computer systems are compatible. Ask the printer how the file is to be formatted; whether the file should come from a Mac (the machine of choice in the book-design world) or PC; what program they will expect you to use for formatting (Quark Xpress is common, but not the first choice for the home publisher because of its expense and level of sophistication); how the fonts should be supplied; and anything else relevant to capturing and delivering the files correctly.

Paper – Text
There seem to be about a million types of paper to use in printing a book, from the finest, whitest, heaviest virginal vellum to coarse, recycled newsprint.

Many books use a stock similar to the one used in this book: a good serviceable choice that is easy on the eyes without costing the earth. If this is a good choice for you, tell your printer you're looking for a 50 lb. white stock. If you want something grander, you will have a wealth of choice up to 120 lb. If you have seen an existing book with paper that you admire and want for your book, it's probably best to supply your printer with a copy of the book and let the staff try to figure out what has been used or what's available that is similar.

The real issues for you may be the use of recycled paper and the acidity of the paper. If you want to use recycled paper, simply tell your printer. Paper acidity became a hot topic a few years ago when the danger of paper deterioration in modern

TYPICAL PRINTING COSTS

Some typical costs for printing home-published books at a book manufacturing plant:

Book	Size	Page count	Printing and binding	Quantity	Rough Cost
Local history	8 x 10"	160 pages	text in black; cover in colour; softcover	1000 copies	$7000
Cookbook	7 x 10"	128 pages	text in black; cover in colour; softcover	1000 copies	$3500
Children's Storybook	8 x 8"	32 pages	text and cover printed in full colour; softcover	1000 copies	$3500
Novel	6-1/4 x 9"	320 pages	text in black; cover in colour; softcover	1000 copies	$4500
Self-Help	5-1/2 x 8-1/2"	128 pages	text in black; cover in colour; softcover	2000 copies	$3300

Assumes same weight of paper (50 lb. offset) used for all the books and their covers (10 pt.). Note: No category has been provided for hardcover because hardcover books are very costly to produce. If you can afford such a book, you should probably pay a book designer to manage the production of the project.

books in libraries and other collections was first recognized. Paper manufacturers responded to this concern by producing acid-free book papers, and now most book paper is acid-free. If you want your book to last long after you do, specify acid-free paper to be sure that's what you're getting.

Paper – Cover

You have already determined whether you are making a cover or a jacket, but let's quickly review: a cover is the heavy printed paper encasing the pages of a softcover book, while a jacket wraps around the case of a hardcover book. You will probably choose to produce a softcover book.

Softcover books make large use of a stock called Cornwall, coated one side (C1S); the stock is virtually always 10 pt. or 12 pt., the latter being slightly heavier than the former and, correspondingly, slightly more expensive.

Covers are virtually always finished with a plastic lamination on their printed side. This coating provides a pleasant-looking sheen to the cover while also helping to protect the cover from getting dirty and torn.

Hardcover Materials – Case, Jacket and Endpapers

Case. There are so many different ways to produce a case for a book that it is impossible to describe what might or might not be a good choice. For starters, you will need to specify natural or synthetic materials. Printers have sample books showing these materials. You will need to see these samples to make your choice unless you are providing a sample of what you like and use that as your quotation reference point. On your Request for Quotation, put "See attached sample."

Jacket. Jacket paper is usually quite substantial in weight; jackets, after all, take a beating. Many publishers now avoid hardcover books, because they cost so much to produce, and once the jackets are damaged, which always seems to happen the instant the books hit the stores, the books are unsaleable. Specify a 100 lb. gloss stock for the jacket and you will have a handsome jacket on your book.

Endpapers. An endpaper is the plain or patterned paper you see when you open a hardcover book. Endpapers can be white, uniformly coloured, printed or individually created by use of specialized techniques such as marbleizing. A 100 lb. offset stock will do nicely for endpapers unless you are going to create them yourself. If you are going this route, tell your printer and follow the directions for what you will need to supply to ensure the correct size and general suitability.

Printing – Text
Ever heard a book described as being printed in black and white? It's a common description for a book that is actually printed in black ink; the white, of course, is provided by the colour of the paper.

Remember then that the colour of the paper is an element for consideration. White paper will support all colour choices; a neutral-coloured paper — cream, for instance — will support the use of single dark colours, such as dark green or blue, but not four colours. A coloured stock in any strong colour (dark turquoise, neon pink, orange) is best not used.

Your choices in printing, while some would describe them as limitless, are actually a choice of:
• black
• specially coloured inks called PMS colours
• four-process colours
• a combination of four-process colours with PMS colours (rare in the commercial book world)

You must tell the printer which one of these formats you plan to use. (See page 133 for a quick explanation of colour printing processes.)

You will also need to specify whether your text pages have a "bleed"; it is always assumed by the printer that the cover or jacket will bleed, and they are quoted accordingly. A bleed is a rather unfortunate choice of words to describe whether the printing goes right to the edge of the page, or not. A full-colour photograph, for instance, that covers the entire page of the book, without any white margin showing around the outside edges, is said to bleed. If even one line across the top of the text runs off the edge, that is a bleed. Pages with a bleed can cost more to print than those without, because it may mean the printer needs to use a larger sheet of paper. If there is no bleed on your pages, you must restrict your printing within the margins set by the printer; usually these are not less than 1/4" to 3/8". It's wise to leave a greater margin than this in any case, to ensure that your print doesn't come perilously close to the edge of the page.

A QUICK PRIMER ON COLOUR

Colour on a printed page is achieved in one of two ways. To print a colour image, such as a colour photo, that photo must first be electronically scanned and broken down into its constituent parts of blue (cyan), magenta (red), yellow and black. This is called colour separation. A colour image, such as a photo, will be printed in dots of the four separate colours — blue, magenta, yellow and black. This is called four-colours process. Various combinations of these dots can yield an infinite number of colours. Coloured type will either be printed four-colours process or by using specified PMS (Pantone Matching System) colours. PMS is specially premixed inks available for printers' use in an enormous array of colours, including neons and metallics. To print type in two colours it is far less expensive to use PMS colour than four-colours process.

If you use PMS colours in addition to four-colours process, which is possible in order to produce a book with six, eight or even the virtually unheard-of, twelve-colour printing, you'll be entering the stratosphere in the expense department.

Four-colours process printing is very expensive because it requires, first of all, the scanning of the colour photographs (which can cost upwards of $50 per photo), second, the production of one sheet of film for each colour for every page in the book, with colour proofs of suffi-cient quality to be used during print as checks for colour, and, finally, one printing plate for each colour. Even though printers are now intro-ducing direct-to-plate four-colour technology, thereby eliminating the need for film, four-colour printing will continue to be a costly method of reproduction.

Achieving colour in a book using PMS colours is much less expen-sive. Less film is needed and fewer plates are required. Book printers have been using direct-to-plate technology for two-colour printing for some time. This saves the expense of producing a sheet of film of each colour for every page in the book.

In order to specify what PMS colour or colours you want to use, you will need to consult with your printing rep to see the PMS book dis-playing all the colours available. Usually the colours are shown printed on a coated stock, where they appear bright and lively, and on an uncoated stock, where they appear dull in comparison. Just be aware that, if you pick a colour from the coated portion of the book and you're printing on uncoated paper, you're going to be disappointed with the result. Each ink colour in the PMS system has a code number. Record this number to specify it on your purchase order to your printer.

Printing – Cover

It is much more cost efficient to produce a book printed in black for the text and then inject a strong dose of colour on the cover. Again, you must specify four-colours process, PMS or a combination (rare) and be prepared to deliver materials to the printer accordingly.

If you are printing four-colours process, many publishers choose to deliver film for the job. In order to deliver film, you must work with a printing film supply house in order to achieve the correct output for the printer.

If your cover is making exclusive use of PMS colour, you might choose to deliver the cover on disk. Before doing this, check with the printer to see what kind of disk is acceptable and what is needed both on the disk (fonts for instance) and with the disk (an inkjet colour print, for instance). Delivering what the printer needs to do the job properly will make the whole production process easier for you and for the printer.

Hardcover Printing – Cases, Jacket and Endpapers

Cases. As previously discussed, manufacturing cases is a complicated procedure. So is their printing. Cases can be printed in four colours and laminated or foil stamped on the front and spine. You already know the demands that four-colour work places on the designer and home publisher. Stamping is fairly easily accomplished by providing the printer with the art in a format from which they can make film and, subsequently, a stamping die. You simply need to specify the colour of foil to be used.

Jackets. Jackets are virtually always printed in four-colours process, or even four-colours process plus PMS. They're pretty lavish productions, and if you're putting a jacket on your book, you might as well go all out and print four colours too. Specify four-colours process plus 1/2 mil gloss lamination to provide a nice finish and add durability.

Endpapers. Endpapers can be white or printed in one or more PMS colours or four-colours process. They can also be hand-made by you or you can purchase beautiful handmade endpapers through your printer. Assess what suits your vision and your budget.

Binding

You have a number of binding options available through your printer. The following table helps to show what binding is best for each size of book.

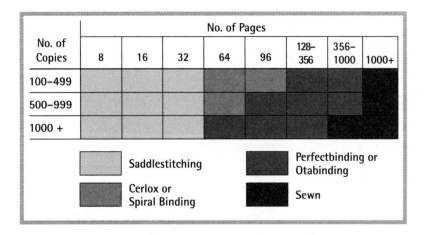

No. of Copies	No. of Pages							
	8	16	32	64	96	128–356	356–1000	1000+
100–499								
500–999								
1000 +								

Saddlestitching

Cerlox or Spiral Binding

Perfectbinding or Otabinding

Sewn

Saddlestitching. As previously described, this kind of binding involves stapling through the centre of the pages. Two or three staples are customary.

This is really appropriate for — and sometimes the only option available with — books having 64 pages or fewer. Withstands fairly rugged use. Inexpensive.

Cerlox or Spiral Binding. Cerlox is a plastic ring binding in which each ring is separate from the other rings. It comes in a few standard colours and the spine edge of the Cerlox rings can be printed. Can be used for books of up to about 450 pages. Not durable, and not the best looking binding. Inexpensive.

When a book is wiro-bound or spiral bound, a continuous wire is woven through the spine edge of the pages to hold the book together. The wire can be coloured or clear and, like Cerlox binding, can be used with a few pages or many pages.

Often used in self-published cookbooks because it allows the book to lie flat when in use. Durable and costly.

Perfectbinding and Otabinding. Perfectbinding glues together the spine and the cover. There is a minimum number of pages that can be bound this way that varies somewhat from printer to printer, but is usually not less than 64 pages. The maximum is about 1,200 pages, but this depends on the weight of stock used. Perfectbinding is durable and relatively inexpensive. Despite the fact that the pages can snap shut when the book is opened, and the spine can become brittle with age, causing pages to drop out, perfectbinding is used for all kinds of books and is the most common method of binding today.

Otabinding is the trade name for a type of perfectbinding in which a thin piece of fabric attached to the glue on the spine means the spine has a greater degree of flex. This allows the book pages to lie flatter when opened.

Sewn. A sewn binding literally stitches together the sections, or forms, of the book. It produces a binding that is highly durable. The pages are easy to open, lie flat when opened and won't drop out. Sewn binding is used mostly for reference books, in which long life is important, cookbooks and some children's books. To be sewn, a book must be constructed of more than one form, or section, or else there would be nothing to stitch together. Make sure your book has at least 64 pages before specifying sewn binding. Expensive compared to other forms of binding.

Finished Book Date

Your need for your book may be predicated on a certain event: a conference, for instance, at which you plan to sell the book. Otherwise, you may only have a fair idea of when you'd like it — say, in plenty of time for Christmas.

Either way, you should specify a date to the printer. Whether the printer can achieve or maintain this date will depend almost entirely on you. If you have contacted the company on December 2 for your Christmas book, you're out of luck and the printer will advise you accordingly. If, however, you have planned three months or so in advance, you will have a good chance of meeting that date.

Maintaining the schedule to keep delivery on track is your job. Don't expect the printer to make up time you have lost. But if you have promised to deliver your materials as of a certain date, and you have fulfilled your part of the bargain, then the printing company should meet its commitment accordingly.

A SAMPLE REQUEST FOR QUOTATION:

Title:	A Book of One's Own
Quantity:	50,000, 75,000 and 10,0000 copies
Trim size:	5-1/2 x 8-1/2"
Number of pages:	192
Paper: Text:	50 lb. Hibulk, white
Paper: Cover:	10 pt. Cornwall C1S
Printing: Text:	One colour black
Printing: Cover:	Four-colours process with 1/2 mil gloss lamination one side only
Preparation: Text:	Text copy as Quark Xpress files on disk, Macintosh format, including all screen and printer fonts, to printer's specifications. Printer to output disk files to film. Laser proofs to accompany text files.
Preparation: Cover:	Comprehensive colour separated cover negatives imposed to printer's specification.
Binding:	Perfectbound
Delivery:	To one address in the Greater Toronto area
Taxes:	Additional

Shipping

You must decide whether your printer will be doing the delivery of the finished books or whether you are arranging it. Frankly, unless you're in the business of moving freight, you're better to let the printer look after shipping. If you are printing a sufficient quantity of books that they will be packed in cartons, on skids, make sure your receiving end can accept skids. In other words, moving skids from a transport trailer to your garage isn't going to work.

COMPARING QUOTES

Now you're ready to ask for quotations. When they come in and you've completed your comparisons, you must pick one company with which you will work. Don't try to play companies with competing quotes off one other: you'll only embarrass yourself. Your next step is to issue a purchase order, or letter, confirming your order to your supplier.

Your purchase order or letter should repeat all the specifications in the quotation, as well as the printer's quotation number (if provided). Make sure you include the total cost of all the services you're buying from the printer. A cheque may need to accompany this order; the printer will let you know.

READING THE QUOTES

If you have received competing quotes, take the time to size up the quotations carefully. Make sure that none of the specifications have been changed from your Request for Quote. Also review whether the total cost you're looking at is "all in". Some printers provide one all-inclusive cost, while others provide separate costs for preparation (plates, etc.) and manufacturing. Since both ways of quoting are industry standards, the onus is on you to compare carefully.

You're now ready to gather together the materials you have specified in your purchase order, whether film, disk or hard copy, to allow the printer to begin the job.

THE PURCHASE ORDER FOR THIS BOOK

This is how the purchase order to the printer looked for *A Book of One's Own*:

(Printed on company letterhead.)

To:	Friesens
	212-1370 Don Mills Road
	Don Mills, ON M3B 3N7
Bill to:	Bloomington Books
Ship to:	McClelland & Stewart

RE: A BOOK OF ONE'S OWN: your quote number 00000

Trim size:	5-1/2 x 8-1/2" no bleed in text
Quantity:	x copies
Preparation:	Text copy as Quark Xpress files on disk, Mac format. Laser proofs to accompany text file. Printer to output files to film.
Cover:	Comprehensive colour separated cover negatives imposed to printer's specifications
Paper: Text:	50 lb. Hibulk, white
Cover:	10 pt. C1S
Printing: Text:	Black throughout
Cover:	Four process colours plus 1/2 mil gloss plastic lamination outside only
Overs:	+/- 5% accepted
Binding:	Perfectbound
Delivery Date:	March 12, 1999
Cost:	For x copies @ $x.xx = $
	GST
	Total $

WHAT TO EXPECT WHEN YOU'RE GOING ON PRESS

You've worked with your printer to deliver materials for the text and cover to specifications. Are finished books next?

Not yet. The printer takes what you have supplied and provides you with a set of blueprints or "blues," also sometimes called dyluxes, or vandykes, so you can have one final look-over before going on press. Your signature on the blues is the go-ahead to the printer, so you want to make sure you know what you're looking at and that you are satisfied with what you see.

The blues are a paper proof created from the film. Film is then used to "burn" the printing plates. Blues are in one colour: blue. All the type and all the photos look blue. You can't use blues to check four-colour printing, yet blues will still be created by the printer for pages printed in four colours in recognition that these pages exist.

IT HAPPENS TO THE PROS

There isn't be a person in publishing who doesn't have a horror story about a mistake caught at the blues stage. One of our favourites concerns a cookbook with a 50,000 copy print run being prepared for a very demanding author, which was found in blues to be missing its title page. With the error discovered mere hours before going on press, a title page had to be created, film produced and transported in the middle of the night from the film house to the publisher, who waited on the side of a lonely highway to take the film to the waiting printer. The moral: It happens. But, it doesn't need to if proper thought, time and care are taken in the preparation of the book.

Because blues are produced from the film, which is one of the final stages in the printing process, it will be expensive at this point to make corrections. Every change will mean new film, and that cost adds up fast. Plus, you will lose time in creating new film, and you can lose your place in the printing queue if the process starts to drag.

So, though it may be hard to restrain yourself, looking at blues is not the time to reread the book for grammatical errors, typos or a general change of heart. That happened in Chapter 4. Blues are, however, your opportunity to do many tasks that seem pretty obvious:

- ensure all the pages are there and that they are in the right order;
- ensure all the elements that comprise each page are there: the running head or foot, folio, all the text, captions if there are any and illustrations or photos;
- ensure that there are no scratch marks, blobs of dirt or hairs on the type or illustrations, that the type is not broken; and
- ensure that all the elements for the cover are in place.

Usually the printer will supply an approval page on which you can list those pages where something has caught your eye that needs attention. Do this; it also helps to mark directly on the blue page with a big circle around the offending item, in red ink, grease pencil or china marker, what you want the printer to check on the film.

The reality is that it is difficult to consistently look at page after page without reading the text. So, it is really important to go through the blues two or three times, each time focussing on the pages and the type without being distracted by the story.

> **DON'T READ THIS UPSIDE DOWN!**
>
> It helps to review blues from back to front as well as from front to back, because, if your attention wanders once or twice as you go along, you know you will have really seen the end of the book too. And it also helps to look at the blues upside down. This guarantees that you won't be reading the words but that you will be looking at the elements of each page.

If all is satisfactory, it's off to press. Off to press means patience. Printers' schedules have been known to move printing to an earlier time slot, but far more frequently they move back. If you have been given a finished book date, and you should have been given this in your discussions with the printer, you'll want to check on the status of the book that day. Many understanding and sympathetic printers might call you to watch your book on press. But, even then, binding does not follow immediately. So, rein in your anxiety, because soon your book will be completed. Then, with your brand-new book in one hand you can pour the champagne with the other and proudly toast your achievement.

CHAPTER 11

FOR THOSE IN A HURRY

Let's say you're in a big hurry for your book, and you want the immediate gratification of making one quickly.

Well, look no further than the following pages. Here is a collection of simple solutions for some of the types of books that home publishers are likely to create. These "quick steps to success" point out how you can combine so many of the ideas that we talk about into your own, custom-made, way of putting all the pieces together.

Don't stop with these ideas! Use them as a springboard to get your creative juices flowing. Combine a page-making technique from here, with a binding from there, to come up with an individual answer to your individual need.

Enjoy the process. Have fun! Make one book before you make 100, or ten or, even, five, to get the kinks out, and then, go to it!

QUICK: IT'S A KID'S BOOK!

> ## DESIRED OUTCOME
>
> You want to preserve a story you've written for your child, or that your child has written for you. You know the grandparents will be rapturous, and that nieces and nephews, too, will enjoy the simple story accompanied by the crayon drawings that help to tell the story. When it's complete, you just might send along a copy to that children's publishing company from whom you buy so many books. This is a project for fun, that will cost very little and not be terribly time-consuming. You plan for:
>
> | | |
> |---|---|
> | book size: | 7 x 7" |
> | number of pages: | 16 |
> | number of copies: | 25 |
> | layout: | the story will be printed in black and the drawings in colour |

MAKING PAGES ON THE COMPUTER

1. If you're using a computer to make up pages, set the type according to the typefaces suggested in the table on page 80.

2. Use the grid on page 183 to establish margins; modify it to the 7 x 7" size.

3. Using the computer, make up the pages in a computer word-processing program in printer's spreads, see p. 105, and place all the story type. Make sure you insert a small mark at the top, middle and bottom of the page where the centre fold line will be to assist in even folding later, and at the tops and bottoms of each page, so that they can be evenly trimmed to the finished size.

4. Print out one set of pages on 8-1/2 x 14" paper, check carefully and make any final type adjustments.

5. Scan in the drawings, or use a supplier to do the scans. Position them according to the grid.

6. Print out one full set of pages. When OK, if you have a colour printer, print out 25 sets of pages. If you do not have a colour printer, take them to a copy shop, business supply outlet, or other supplier to print. Continue as instructed under "Putting the Book Together".

MAKING PAGES WITHOUT A COMPUTER

1. Use the grid on page 183 to establish margins; modify it to the 7 x 7" size. Draw the guidelines for the grid onto the paper you will be using to create the original set of book pages, using a non-reproducing blue pencil (available through a graphic-arts supply store). You must make the pages in printer's spreads, see p. 105. Make sure you insert a small mark at the top, middle and bottom of the page where the centre fold line will be to assist in even folding later, and at the tops and bottoms of each page so that they can be evenly trimmed to the finished size.

2. Use your very best handwriting to print the story onto the pages where you've drawn your grid following the directions in Chapter 8.

3. Paste the drawings into position.

4. Take this original to a photocopy shop for colour copying. Continue as instructed under "Putting the Book Together".

PUTTING THE BOOK TOGETHER

1. Design your front cover by pasting a drawing into a centre panel on the front cover and position the title above the drawing and the author's name below.

2. Photocopy 25 front covers on 8-1/2 x 11" white bond. Trim the copies to the 7 x 7" size. Cut 25 pieces of card stock or Bristol board to just a hair larger than 7 x 14". Paste each front cover colour copy onto that portion of the Bristol board that will become the front cover when the book is closed. Apply GEO Multi Fix Adhesive Film to the whole cover — front and back on the outside — or, to economize, just the front cover, for a nice glossy finish. Score covers (see p. 109) on their inside, down the middle, to make folding easier.

3. Use a sharp utility knife and a straight-edge on a firm surface to trim the pages down to the 7 x 14" size.

4. Wrap covers around pages; staple three times down the centre fold through all thicknesses. Fold into closed books.

5. Using the knife and straight-edge again, trim off the any excess paper that may be protruding along the front edge of the book. A copy shop or small printer can also do the trimming of the pages, covers and finished books for you.

TIP

If you're creating the colour pages from your own printer, buy a new colour cartridge before starting in order to ensure even colour throughout all copies.

MY POEMS ARE PUBLISHED

DESIRED OUTCOME

This is one of the most personal of all the types of books created by the home publisher. Chances are you'll be very satisfied with a few copies: one for yourself and one each for your nearest and dearest. This is a project in which you've already put so much of yourself into the writing that you'll probably want to carry the same level of intensity through production of the book. Your plan includes:

book size:	5 x 8"
number of pages:	64
number of copies:	10
layout:	the poems will be printed in black

MAKING PAGES ON THE COMPUTER

1. If you're using a computer to make up pages, set your type according to the typefaces suggested in the table on page 80.
2. Use the grid on page 180 to establish margins; modify it to the 5 x 8" size.
3. Make up the pages in a computer word-processing program, see p. 105.
4. Print out one set of pages on 8-1/2 x 11" paper, check carefully that each page is properly backed up and make any final type adjustments.
5. Print out one full set of pages on the finest quality paper that your computer printer will accept. Cream-coloured, heavy-weight stock would be a good choice. Print out ten sets of pages. If the printer can't handle this kind of paper, or any other that you have your heart set on using, print an original

set of pages on laser paper, and take these, with the paper you've chosen for the inside pages, to a copy shop, business-supply outlet or other supplier to photocopy. Continue as instructed under "Putting the Book Together".

MAKING PAGES WITHOUT A COMPUTER

1. Use the grid on page 180 to establish margins; modify it as necessary to the 5 x 8" size. Draw the guidelines for the grid onto the paper you will be using to create the original set of book pages, using a non-reproducing blue pencil (available through a graphic-arts supply store).

2. Use your very best handwriting to write or print the poems on the pages where you've drawn your grid.

3. Take the one complete set of pages with the paper you've chosen for the inside pages — if it is a specialty stock — to a copy shop, business-supply outlet or other supplier to photocopy. If using standard paper, the copy shop will supply the paper and include its cost with the cost of photocopying. Continue as instructed under "Putting the Book Together".

PUTTING THE BOOK TOGETHER

1. Have all the pages trimmed to the 5 x 8" size at the copy shop or at a small commercial printer.

2. Find a beautiful heavyweight paper for the cover, such as a handmade paper. If your choice is fairly flimsy, glue this paper onto a card-weight stock or Bristol board that will serve to stiffen it. Make ten front covers. Using a utility knife and a straight

edge on a firm surface, trim the covers to the size of the finished book. "Tip-in" your type as suggested on page 55. Use another ten sheets of either the card-weight stock or Bristol board for the back cover, and also trim these to the 5 x 8" size.

3. Put the covers on the front and back of each set of book pages. Punch holes through all the pages with their covers as described in the method for Japanese binding, page 113. Handsew using embroidery thread.

A NOVEL IDEA

DESIRED OUTCOME

After the rave reviews your friends, co-workers, members of the reading club and the writer-in-residence gave you, you're shooting for the moon with your book. You have the confidence in its sales power — and the money! — to do the book production job using the experts. Since your heart is set on a large print run, you'll be going the offset printing route.

book size:	6 x 9"
number of pages:	320
number of copies:	2,000
layout:	the text will be printed in black, the cover will be printed in four colours

---

METHOD

1. You locate a book designer through your local community college, which offers a book arts program. You hire the designer to do both text and cover designs. You deliver your text file to the designer in a word-processing application file.

2. Meanwhile, you locate three companies that can print the book. You devise your specifications with the sales reps and request quotes.

3. After comparing costs, you decide to use the company that offers free storage for the books for six months after printing and proceed to issue a purchase order with the portion of payment you've negotiated up front.

4. The designer submits ideas for the cover, and a sample of how the inside pages will look. You work with the designer to make changes you think are

important. You write the back cover copy and give it to the designer.

5. The designer supplies a set of all the book pages for checking. You mark a number of changes, and the designer supplies a revised set of pages. These are approved by you.

6. The designer submits a final design of the cover, including the spine and back cover, for your approval.

7. The designer prepares and sends an electronic file (Syquest or e-mail) of the text for the printer.

8. Another electronic file is prepared for the cover. This is sent to a film supply company. They will make film and show you colour proofs for approval. Then they send the film and proofs to the printer.

9. The printer shows you a proof of the electronic text file, then prints and binds the books.

DOWN MEMORY LANE

DESIRED OUTCOME

Memoirs, diaries or travel journals are very personal books. The print run is likely to be quite small. Such a book will include maps, photographs and perhaps the series of watercolour sketches made on the author's first trip to Tuscany. As the author, you've got lots of time to give this project, and since it's become your full-time hobby since retirement, you're not afraid to throw some money at it either. You want a very rich-looking book. Your plan includes:

book size:	10 x 8" (binding on the 8" edge)
number of pages:	144
number of copies:	10
layout:	the pages and photos will be printed in black; the watercolours and first page in the book will be printed in full colour

MAKING PAGES ON THE COMPUTER

1. Set your type according to the typefaces suggested in the table on page 80.
2. Use the grid on page 179 to establish margins; modify it as necessary to suit the size of the book.
3. Have your maps and photos supplied as scans or, as you make up the pages in your computer page-making program leave spaces where these pieces of art are to be placed. As you organize the contents, leave full pages blank. This is where the watercolours will appear.
4. Design the first page in the book to include a colour drawing and, perhaps, the title in a smallish box (say 6 x 5"). This will become your cover type.

5. Print out one set of pages on 8-1/2 x 11" paper, check carefully and make any final type adjustments.

6. Prepare a disk according to the requirements of a digital print house. Continue as instructed under "Putting the Book Together".

MAKING PAGES WITHOUT A COMPUTER

1. Use the grid on page 179 to establish margins; modify it as necessary to suit this book size. Draw the guidelines for the grid onto the paper you will be using to create the original set of book pages using a non-reproducing blue pencil (available through a graphic-arts supply store).

2. Use your very best handwriting to write or print the story directly onto the pages where you've drawn your grid. Leave spaces where the photos and watercolours will be placed.

3. Design the first page in the book to include a colour drawing and, perhaps, the title in a smallish box (say 6 x 5"). This will become your cover type.

4. Supply originals of all the text pages and the photos and art to the digital printer with a clear indication of what goes where and what size each is to be printed. Continue as instructed under "Putting the Book Together".

PUTTING THE BOOK TOGETHER

1. The digital printer will show you a proof of all the pages for your approval with the photos and art in position. Once okay, they will print the book and trim it to the finished-book size. The printer can also supply the quantity of covers you need, again trimmed to the finished book size.

2. Choose a 100 lb. matte coated text for the pages. Use a 100 lb. uncoated cover stock, ideally with a linen texture, for the cover, in a dark blue or other colour that coordinates with the colour illustration on page 1. Die-cut each cover with a box to correspond to the box on the first book page. If you feel your die-cutting isn't up to scratch, take the covers to a shop where they frame art. If they cut mattes for framing, they can cut your covers.

3. Punch holes in each set of pages with their covers using a small awl as described in the method for Japanese binding, page 113. Handsew using embroidery thread in a colour that complements the cover.

THE COLLECTED RECIPES OF...

> ### DESIRED OUTCOME
>
> The volunteer group at the hospital wants to produce a book of recipes that they will sell through the gift shop and to all their members to raise money. One "lucky" volunteer has to compile the recipes, and produce the book in her spare time. The book has to be produced inexpensively so that the group can make money from its sales, yet it has to look good enough so that it will sell.
>
> book size: 7 x 10"
> number of pages: 192
> number of copies: 500
> layout: the text will be printed in black,
> the cover will be four colours

MAKING PAGES WITH A COMPUTER

1. Set type according to the typefaces suggested in the table on page 80.
2. Use the grid on page 178.
3. Make up the pages in a computer word-processing program, and place all the type in page format.
4. Using the computer printer, print out one set of pages on 8-1/2 x 11" paper, check carefully and make any final adjustments. When okay, print out one set of pages on laser-quality paper. Continue as instructed under "Putting the Book Together".

MAKING PAGES WITHOUT A COMPUTER

1. Use the grid on page 178 to establish margins; modify it as necessary to suit this book size. Draw the guidelines for the grid onto the paper you will be using to create the original set of book pages using a non-reproducing blue pencil (available through a graphic-arts supply store).

2. Use your very best handwriting to write or print the recipes onto the pages where you've drawn your grid. Continue as instructed under "Putting the Book Together".

PUTTING THE BOOK TOGETHER

1. Hire a book designer to design the cover. Tell the designer this is a four-colour printing job. The designer will submit ideas for the cover for your approval.

2. Upon approval, the designer will prepare the design for the cover and supply it as camera-ready art or an electronic file (Syquest, Zip or e-mail) to either a photocopy shop, a digital printer or a small commercial printer that you have hired to print 500 copies of each of the front and back cover. Don't allow the covers to be trimmed to the finished book size yet.

3. Take your printed covers, and one set of text pages to a photocopy shop. Have the text pages photocopied on good-quality white paper.

4. Then, have the text pages collated with the front and back covers that you supplied. Now, trim the books down to the finished 7 x 10" size. Wiro-bind

the books at your photocopy shop using a coordi-
nating colour of wire.

> **TIP**
>
> The content of a recipe book is its biggest selling feature. So, while this production route will deliver a good-looking book, the most effort should be put into editing the recipes.

HELP FOR SELF-HELP

DESIRED OUTCOME

You've had a brush with a rare, life-threatening medical condition. Now you want to share your experiences with others. You want to include some really useful information, such as exercises, and even recipes featuring beneficial foods. Circulation will be quite limited, but no one has done a book like this before. This is a project where you want a professional appearance, yet you aren't so convinced of its market potential that you will hire the pros. You decide to do your book like this:

book size:	8-1/2 x 11"
number of pages:	128
number of copies:	250
layout:	the text will be printed in black,
	the cover will be printed in four colours

MAKING PAGES WITH A COMPUTER

1. Set your type according to the typefaces suggested in the table on page 80.

2. Use the grid on page 178 to establish margins.

3. Make up the pages in a computer word-processing program, and place all the type and illustrations that accompany the suggested exercises.

4. Using your computer printer, print out one set of pages on 8-1/2 x 11" paper, check carefully and make any final adjustments. When okay, print out one set of pages. Continue as instructed under "Putting the Book Together".

MAKING PAGES WITHOUT A COMPUTER

1. Use the grid on page 178 to establish margins. Draw the guidelines for the grid onto the paper you will be using to create the original set of book pages using a non-reproducing blue pencil (available through a graphic-arts supply store).

2. Type your manuscript cleanly and carefully onto the grid sheets you prepared.

3. Plan to intersperse full pages of illustrations or photos between full pages of text. Make sure you deal with all the information that would normally be contained in photo captions in the text.

4. Take your photo or art originals to a copy shop or other supplier where you plan to have the pages photocopied and ask them the best way for you to supply these illustrative elements. They may suggest that they will make scans for you, or they might prefer originals. Continue as instructed under "Putting the Book Together".

PUTTING THE BOOK TOGETHER

1. Use a photo or other image on your front cover that is relevant to the group for which the book is being published. Either design the cover on the computer, and print it on a colour laser printer or assemble one by hand. This means you will draw up a cover grid that includes the elements of your cover, and their position. Then you create type for the title and author's name that you will paste onto the grid. You will also have to provide the photo in a format from which the printer can print. Ask

them their preference. Find either a digital printer or a small commercial printer to print 250 covers on a 10 pt cover stock. You will be Cerlox binding (see Tip below), so you only need front covers printed in colour.

2. Design your back cover to be printed in black only. Using your computer printer, print out one good copy, or create one by the cutting and pasting method described above.

3. Take your printed front covers, back cover and one set of text pages to a photocopy shop. Have the back cover photocopied on the heaviest weight of white stock they can use. Have the text pages photocopied on good-quality white paper.

4. Collate the books with the front covers you supplied and then Cerlox bound by the photocopy shop.

> **TIP**
>
> Cerlox binding is a good choice, because it will let the book lie flat for its reader to use while doing the suggested exercises. The book will look more professional because of its full-colour, printed front cover.

THE FAMILY TREE

DESIRED OUTCOME

A family history has many things in common with a memoir, except that it will likely be read by many more people. If you're the person in your family who has taken on the task, you'll need to know how much you can spend on the production: Will you give these books away or sell them? Let's assume you're going to give them away and, as such, you have to work within a fairly tight budget. Your plan includes:

book size: 8-1/2 x 11"

number of pages: 256

number of copies: 25

layout: the pages and photos will be printed in black;
                  the cover will be in colour.

MAKING PAGES ON THE COMPUTER

1. Set your type according to the typefaces suggested in the table on page 80.

2. Use the grid on page 178 to establish margins.

3. You decide to organize the book into text pages (the story) and photo pages, which will be grouped together in sections to create the feel of a photo album.

4. Print out one set of text pages on 8-1/2 x 11" paper, check carefully and make any final type adjustments. Photocopy these pages.

5. Scan in the photos, or have them scanned; lay them out in pages and print 25 sets of these pages on special "photography" type paper on a laser printer. Continue as instructed under "Putting the Book Together".

MAKING PAGES WITHOUT A COMPUTER

1. Use the grid on page 178 to establish margins. Draw the guidelines for the grid onto the paper you will be using to create the original set of book pages using a non-reproducing blue pencil (available through a graphic-arts supply store).
2. Type your manuscript cleanly and carefully onto the grid sheets you prepared. Photocopy these pages.
3. Plan to intersperse several full pages of photos at intervals between full pages of text in a photo-album treatment. It is normal to deal with all the information that would normally be contained in photo captions in the text.
4. Take your photos to a copy shop or other supplier where you will have the pages photocopied and ask them the best way for you to supply these illustrative elements. They may suggest that they will make scans for you, or they might prefer originals. Have them photocopy 25 sets of the photo pages, ideally on a photo-quality paper, if their machine can handle this special stock. Continue as instructed under "Putting the Book Together".

PUTTING THE BOOK TOGETHER

1. Insert the photo-section pages among the text pages, as planned. Three-hole punch all the pages, being very careful to always have the holes in exactly the same spot.
2. Either design the cover on the computer, and print it on a colour laser printer or assemble one by hand. This means you will draw up a cover grid that

includes the elements of your cover, and their position. Then you create type for the title and author's
name that you will paste onto the grid. You will
also have to provide any illustration that you plan to
include on the cover, in a format from which the
printer can print. Ask them their preference. Make
25 colour laser prints or colour photocopies.

3. Find a heavy-weight card stock, such as white
Bristol board, and cut 50 pieces: each one needs to
be 10 x 11" for the type of binding you will do.
Score (see page 109) each cover — front and back
— along the 10" side, 1-1/2" from the edge. When
that "lip" is folded in, your cover sheets will be
8-1/2 x 11" and will correspond to the size of your
text pages. Three-hole punch that narrow lip on all
the covers. Paste the photocopies of your cover art
onto the sheets that will become the front covers.

4. Fold each lip with the holes to the back on the
front covers, and the front on the back covers. Align
the holes with the holes in the text pages. Insert a
brass fastener through the holes and then close the
covers (the covers will hide the fasteners).

TIP

If you don't mind whether the fastener shows on the back cover, you
can simply cut the sheets to the 8-1/2 x 11" size without making the
"lip" and three-hole punch them on the 11" edge.

CHAPTER 12

TO MARKET?
TO MARKET!

There are no mysteries when it comes to how a book is sold. But it may seem so to someone outside the book-publishing world. So, we are going to talk about the process of convincing, or selling, the people who have the power to market, market, market.

HOW BOOKS ARE SOLD

The process of selling a book goes something like this: author to agent to publisher to sales reps to market. You may think you want to leapfrog directly from author to market, because you have self-published your book, but let's think some more about this.

You tried unsuccessfully to find a publisher for your book. The point remains: You probably don't know why you were turned down. It's possible that the publisher didn't like your book, but there are a variety of other reasons your book could have been rejected. Consider:

- Most publishers don't accept unsolicited manuscripts. If you just sent yours in, chances are good it wasn't even read.

- Perhaps the publisher already has more on their plate than their resources can handle. Good as your book is, they just can't fit it in.
- Possibly the publishers didn't see the uniqueness of the book, of which you, as its author, are very aware.

You now have at your disposal a rebuttal to all of these objections. You can take your manuscript and, using the advice in these pages, produce a professional-looking book. By sending a finished book to a publisher, you have already made their life easier because so many of the production steps, such as editing and proofreading, have already been completed. You are then in a position to re-solicit a publisher, but this time with an eye to distribution. Distribution can be achieved by packaging the book for the publisher, in which case you will reprint your book for the publisher to their specifications and including their logo, name, ISBN and imprint *or* you can seek a straight distribution deal.

BOOK PACKAGING

Publishers like book packagers because they need them. Book packagers provide product. If that sounds cold, it's because we have now entered the realm of the book *business*.

Packagers presell books to publishers. They pitch an idea for a book that will be delivered at a predetermined price for a set quantity, according to the publisher's schedule. In this way, publishers pick up good books at a price that allows them to make their "margins" without having to increase their in-house resources to do so. After all, there are only so many books a publisher can produce with on-hand staff. But, a publisher can acquire packaged books without seriously affecting the in-house contingent. This is called "adding to the list".

Packagers usually have one ace up their particular sleeves: they're insiders. They know the publishers, the editors, the sales managers, the presidents of the publishing houses. Packagers have access.

As a home publisher, it's not just that you don't know these people. After all, their names and phone numbers are easy enough to find. What is important is that they don't know you.

You can change this. You can produce a limited run of your book — just enough to send a copy to each of the decision-makers at the publishing houses that best suit your book. Make sure you include the sales and marketing people on your mailing list. It's important to recognize in your selling process that not all publishers sell to all people. There are children's book specialists, cookbook specialists, fiction specialists and general non-fiction specialists, among others. Be sure you try to deal only with the houses that could be interested in your work. The books listed on page 7, not only list publishers and key personnel, but also indicate the subjects each tends to publish.

When you send a copy of your book, make sure you back it up with professional-looking sales information, such as a review of competitive works and points of differentiation. Use hard facts and statistics to point out the size of the potential market. You will need to offer a cost to the publisher. Provide a cost for 2,000 copies — regardless of what you believe the size of the market truly to be — that is about 20% to 25% of the proposed retail selling price. If the proposed selling price is $19.95, your cost to the publisher will need to be between $4.00 and $5.00.

You may be shocked that you will receive so little, but the math is simple. If the retail selling price of the book is established at $19.95, because that is the price the market will bear for this type of book, retailers will keep between 40% and 50% of the selling price for their efforts and the publisher will receive the balance — about $10 to $12. This is called the net price. The net price has to pay the cost of distribution — invoicing, shipping, warehousing — which is often pegged at 40% of the net price. That accounts for another $4.00. This now leaves $6.00 of the original $19.95 for the publisher. Of this, the publisher needs to allow for returns of unsold books (bookstores can return 100% of the books they buy), pay the packager, factor in overhead expenses and make a profit. This lesson proves that you will actually be very lucky to get $5.00 for your book: The publisher may only be able to offer less. So, if the $19.95 retail price works for the publisher, and you are prepared to accept the offer the publisher makes for your book, factoring in all the changes you might have to make to the book to meet the publisher's requirements, you just might hammer out a deal. If the $19.95 price won't work because, for instance, you need to receive $7.00 for every book to pay the costs you're incurring, then a deal isn't likely.

Should you accept any offer the publisher makes? You may be tempted to decline, because you believe your book is worth more, and that you will earn far more in royalties as an author.

At this point you've come full circle: How do you convince the publisher to make you an author and add your book to the company list?

THE DISTRIBUTION OPTION

Another option is to convince a publisher to distribute the book. In this case, you will provide the publisher with copies of the book at a negotiated discount from the retail selling price. You will be paid for copies sold and will bear the cost for returned books. The publisher will assume sales, marketing and promotion costs.

Be prepared for the hefty discount the publisher-as-distributor will expect. They will keep about 70% of the net price of the book, and you will receive the balance. But, don't look at this as if you're giving away the farm. For the money you pay the distributor, you're gaining expert help, warehousing, a catalogue listing, the benefits of a full-time national sales force representing your book to achieve widespread distribution and order fulfillment.

THE CANADIAN BOOKSELLERS' ASSOCIATION CONVENTION

Every year Canadian booksellers gather at their annual convention in June, held alternately in Toronto and Vancouver. The convention features booths of the publishing houses hyping their big fall releases. Booksellers from across the country attend to see what's on offer from every publisher at the show — and to keep up with the latest news and gossip.

You might want to attend the show for many reasons. You'll get a much better feel for which publisher specializes in what types of books, and you may find a few names you didn't know. Also you'll have a great opportunity to chat with booksellers and shmooze with publishers to gently sound them out on their reactions about what you have to offer.

Although the CBA is not considered a "selling fair" (the order books are kept under wraps), it is a forum where people in the business can meet. If you can begin the process of making a sale, all the better.

Or, you can convince one of the country's independent book sales organizations to represent your book. You can find the names of these agencies through one of the publishing associations (see Chapter 2).

These organizations usually pick up lines of books from abroad to represent in this country. They are insiders and know who to talk to, when and why.

Good, locally produced books can add to their list, the same way that such books add to the lists of publishing houses.

You will have to negotiate a selling price, terms and a returns policy with such a firm. They will provide all the services offered by a publishing house in return for about 70% of the net price of the book.

STRAIGHT TO THE SELLER

Your other option is to dispense with the pros entirely and go it alone. Doing this means sacrificing their expertise and access to every market where books are sold — chain and independent bookstores, public and private libraries, book clubs, university and college bookstores, specialty retailers such as gift stores and the warehouse clubs (such as Costco). You are going to market the book yourself.

First, you must make sure your book has the technical necessities: an ISBN and bar code on the back. Without these, stores won't touch the book.

Then, you will have to meet the buyer for each distribution channel: stores, libraries, warehouse clubs, etc. You will have to find out who the right buyer is, because buying in bookstores and libraries is often differentiated by genre. You must be prepared with the following information:

- Your terms of sale: What discount are you offering? When do you expect to be paid — 30 days, 90 days, 120 days?
- Promotion or publicity: What are you offering? Will you be advertising the book? Are you prepared to pay the cost of advertising the book in their promotional flyer?

- Returns: how will you handle them? Are you prepared to take the books back? And, to add insult to
injury, will you pay for the shipping cost on the
returns?

Yes, it's a tough business. Even worse, if you do manage to place
the book, because you are a one-book operation, you will be
on the bottom of the pile when it comes to getting paid.
Regardless of the terms negotiated, you are not in a position of
strength or influence. At that point, you can learn the job of
collections in addition to your job as book publisher, because
you're going to be doing that too.

Is there an easier way? There is if your sales expectations are
modest and you're willing to work hard.

STRAIGHT TO THE BUYERS

Analyze who is going to buy that book you've worked so hard
to make. Identify one or two likely groups of people, and then
think about how you can avoid the "big guys" in the retail frenzy

---

PLAY IT SAFE

Horror stories abound about self-publishers who financed the cost of
producing a large print run of books by taking out hefty bank loans, or
otherwise borrowing money. Don't fall into this trap. Plan your book so
that you can pay for its cost from your cash on hand.

One of the big culprits in driving costs up is a print run that is far
too large for a first printing. It just can't be emphasized enough that
books are tough to sell. Be very conservative about how many books you
print so that, when the books come in, you can pay all the bills yourself.
Then, you can tackle how to sell them with a clear head and not a
cleared-out bank account!

and get your book into the hands of those who will really appreciate it. While you're thinking about who is going to sell the book, think too about how you are going to support their efforts through promotion or publicity.

Be Creative in Your Thinking...

A local history could sell to the local libraries and at local gift shops, service stations, tourist attractions, historical societies, independent bookstores and small businesses. If a local event draws a crowd, consider setting up a table and selling the book, or joining forces with another vendor. Get some copies over to the local deejays or TV news hosts, highlighted with a fact sheet of interesting information that they can use to spice up their show.

Poetry is a natural for the New Age shops springing up on main streets across the country. Gift shops, independent bookstores, health-food stores, coffee bars and tourist attractions could also be interested. Consider giving a reading to engage interest.

Children's stories could be sold in toy stores, independent book stores, gift shops and to the local library. Promotion could include free copy giveaways to schools, local dentists, doctors or daycares.

A cookbook could sell in kitchenware shops, the hospital gift shop, independent bookstores and to the local library. An in-store cooking demo works wonders for selling cookbooks, but be prepared to bring everything you need from food, to pans, to serving plates, to paper napkins! Also, be sure to send in some recipes to the local papers, with permission to reprint if credit is given.

Self-help guides sell through logical channels: If the book is based on medical advice, find specific medical associations or self-help groups to sell the book. If there is a convention that brings together the people who would be interested in your book, see if you can reach your potential buyers through the convention and any information directories that such meetings often produce. These groups may be interested in using the book for a fund-raiser, if you can sell it to them at an attractive price. An independent pharmacy might stock the book. A financial guide is more difficult to place: Don't expect banks or trust companies to help out. Your neighbourhood business-supply company, especially if its clientele is small-business oriented, is a more likely choice. Local libraries would also be appropriate. Promotion for this type of book can be challenging. Consider a presentation to a self-help group on a medical issue, or to the local chamber of commerce on a business or financial topic.

Your home-published novel is best placed where people buy books: in bookstores. Send free copies to all the nearby media and really play up the fact that the author is local. Try to find an angle that makes a story of your story.

As an alternative to retail sales, you might instead decide to try a direct-mail campaign by mail or by fax to solicit orders. The most successful direct-mail campaigns have a response rate of about 2%. This means 1,000 pieces of outgoing solicitation by mail or fax might yield as many as 20 book sales. But it's far more likely that you won't do even that well: one book might be it. Don't be too disappointed: such sales results are a function of the method of selling — direct mail/direct fax — and not a reflection on your book.

The Internet has interesting possibilities for selling the book, and as a promotion tool to increase retail sales. You can find appropriate web sites that relate to the content of the book. You'll probably find an e-mail address where you can notify the originator of the site about the book, and even send a sample

THE MECHANICS OF SELLING

Have you thought about how to take orders for your book?

This may be simple in the beginning, because you could literally be selling books from the trunk of your car. Be sure to pack a receipt book with your books so that, as you sell them to each vendor, you can write up a sales receipt. You will, of course, need to acquire a GST number from Revenue Canada first.

On your sales receipt you should indicate who has bought the books, the number of copies they have taken, the per copy price, and the total cost. Most retailers work on a minimum 40% margin, so you should deduct 40% from your suggested retail price to arrive at your selling price to the retailer. In other words, you would sell a $19.95 book to the store for $11.97 a copy.

Once you have sold books to a store for them to resell to their customers, you will probably want to keep tabs on sales. After a decent interval, contact the person who bought the books from you and inquire how the book is going. A strong rate of sale might mean they need more books; a low rate of sale might mean that you should offer to buy them back.

chapter to be posted on the site (with suitable source information, so that a browser can then track down your book to buy it). Also, let on-line booksellers, such as www.amazon.com or www.chaptersglobe.com know about the book and how they can place orders. Finally, as discussed earlier, you might wish to post your entire book on your own web site. This would be entirely appropriate for a family history, especially if the family is spread around the globe, and just the cost of mailing printed books would be high.

AT THE END OF THE PROCESS

Is selling the book the end of the process? Not at all. In fact, selling the book implies a certain objective that many home publishers never have in mind when they first think about making a book. These are the publishers who will be happy to have produced a book for themselves and their closest friends and family. Their objective in creating a book can be, simply, to enjoy the story or photos more in a traditional format — a book — than if they were not gathered together this way. A book does not have to achieve a certain level of sales to be a valid publication.

And, regardless of whether you write and home publish one book or one hundred, there is a huge degree of satisfaction to be gained by seeing the completion of the writing process in a finished book of one's own.

Sample 8 1/2 x 11" book size professional grid,
binding on 11" edge.

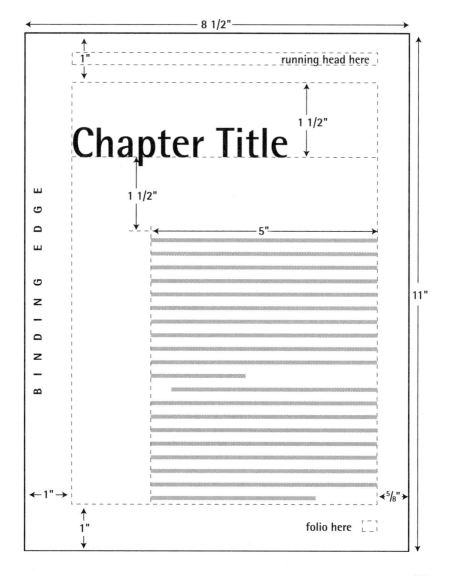

Sample 8 1/2 x 11" book size simple grid,
binding on 11" edge.

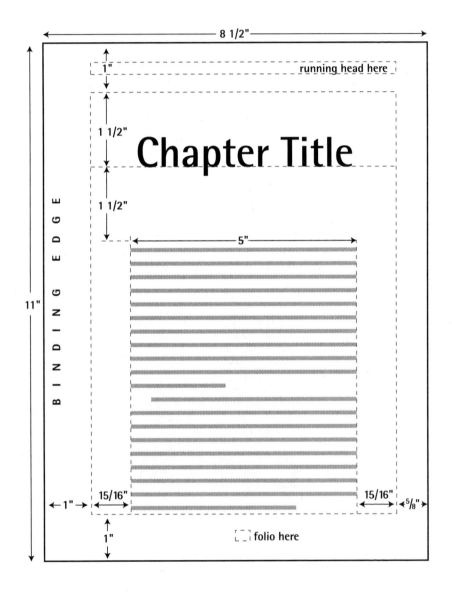

Sample 8 1/2 x 11" book size professional grid,
binding on 8 1/2" edge.

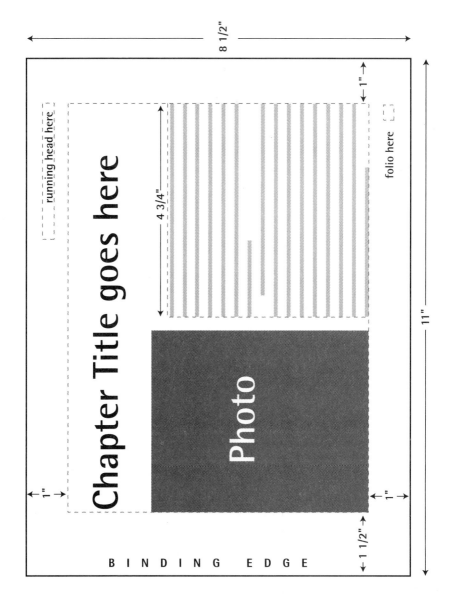

Sample 6 x 9" book size professional grid, binding on 9" edge.

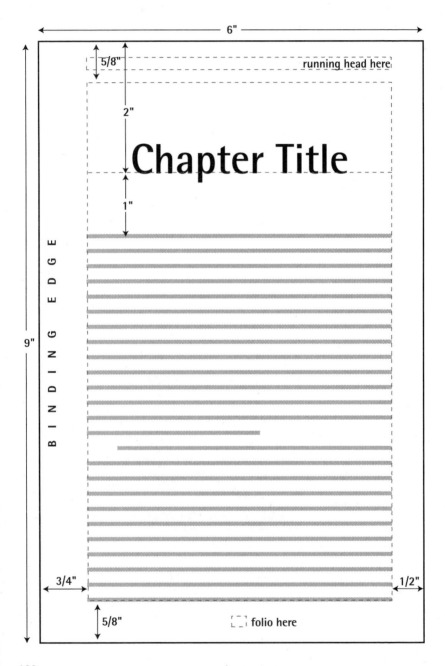

6 x 9" grid continued.

6 x 9" grid continued.

Sample 8 x 8" book size professional grid.

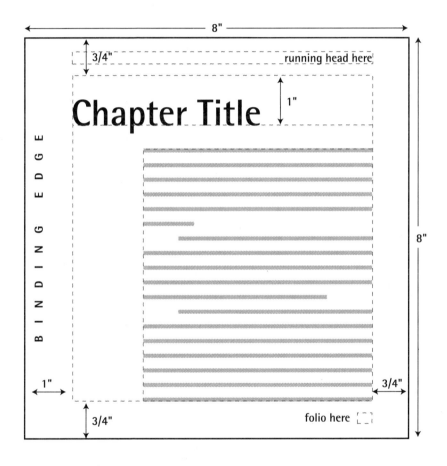

YOUR BOOK TITLE

YOUR NAME

Typeface: Trajan

YOUR BOOK
TITLE

YOUR NAME

Typeface: Trajan

INDEX